Volume 2

easy
GUITAR
play
along

# ACOUSTIC TOP HITS

ISBN 978-1-4584-1581-3

CORPORATION
7777 W. BLUEMOUND RD. P.O. BOX 13819 MILWAUKEE, WI 53213

Visit Hal Leonard Online at
www.halleonard.com

# Guitar Notation Legend

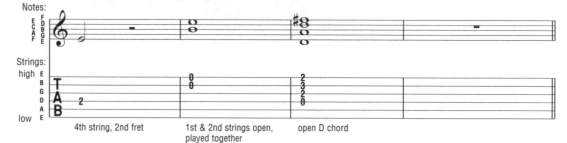

**THE MUSICAL STAFF** shows pitches and rhythms and is divided by bar lines into measures. Pitches are named after the first seven letters of the alphabet.

**TABLATURE** graphically represents the guitar fingerboard. Each horizontal line represents a string, and each number represents a fret.

4th string, 2nd fret          1st & 2nd strings open, played together          open D chord

**HALF-STEP BEND:** Strike the note and bend up 1/2 step.

**WHOLE-STEP BEND:** Strike the note and bend up one step.

**GRACE NOTE BEND:** Strike the note and immediately bend up as indicated.

**SLIGHT (MICROTONE) BEND:** Strike the note and bend up 1/4 step.

**BEND AND RELEASE:** Strike the note and bend up as indicated, then release back to the original note. Only the first note is struck.

**PRE-BEND:** Bend the note as indicated, then strike it.

**VIBRATO:** The string is vibrated by rapidly bending and releasing the note with the fretting hand.

**PALM MUTING:** The note is partially muted by the pick hand lightly touching the string(s) just before the bridge.

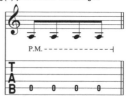

**HAMMER-ON:** Strike the first (lower) note with one finger, then sound the higher note (on the same string) with another finger by fretting it without picking.

**PULL-OFF:** Place both fingers on the notes to be sounded. Strike the first note and without picking, pull the finger off to sound the second (lower) note.

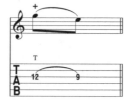

**LEGATO SLIDE:** Strike the first note and then slide the same fret-hand finger up or down to the second note. The second note is not struck.

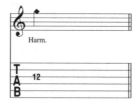

**SHIFT SLIDE:** Same as legato slide, except the second note is struck.

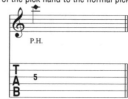

**TRILL:** Very rapidly alternate between the notes indicated by continuously hammering on and pulling off.

**TAPPING:** Hammer ("tap") the fret indicated with the pick-hand index or middle finger and pull off to the note fretted by the fret hand.

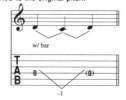

**NATURAL HARMONIC:** Strike the note while the fret-hand lightly touches the string directly over the fret indicated.

**PINCH HARMONIC:** The note is fretted normally and a harmonic is produced by adding the edge of the thumb or the tip of the index finger of the pick hand to the normal pick attack.

**TREMOLO PICKING:** The note is picked as rapidly and continuously as possible.

**VIBRATO BAR DIVE AND RETURN:** The pitch of the note or chord is dropped a specified number of steps (in rhythm), then returned to the original pitch.

**VIBRATO BAR SCOOP:** Depress the bar just before striking the note, then quickly release the bar.

**VIBRATO BAR DIP:** Strike the note and then immediately drop a specified number of steps, then release back to the original pitch.

# Additional Musical Definitions

 *(accent)* • Accentuate note (play it louder).

 *(staccato)* • Play the note short.

***D.S. al Coda*** • Go back to the sign ( 𝄋 ), then play until the measure marked "***To Coda***," then skip to the section labelled "**Coda**."

***D.C. al Fine*** • Go back to the beginning of the song and play until the measure marked "***Fine***" (end).

**Fill** • Label used to identify a brief melodic figure which is to be inserted into the arrangement.

**N.C.** • Harmony is implied.

 • Repeat measures between signs.

• When a repeated section has different endings, play the first ending only the first time and the second ending only the second time.

# About a Girl

**Words and Music by Kurt Cobain**

**Intro**
**Moderately** ♩ = 122

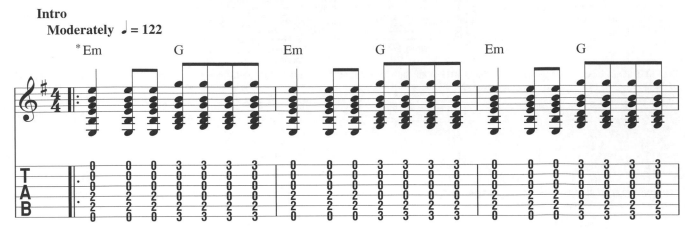

*To match original recording, tune down 1/2 step.

**Verse**

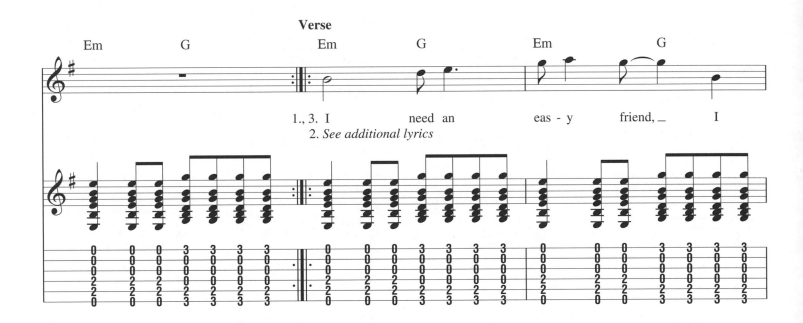

1., 3. I need an eas-y friend, _ I
2. *See additional lyrics*

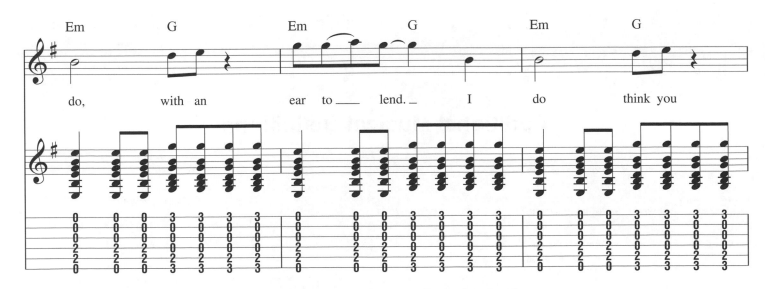

do, with an ear to ___ lend. _ I do think you

**Guitar Solo**

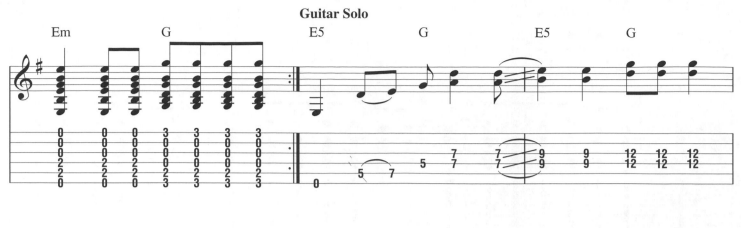

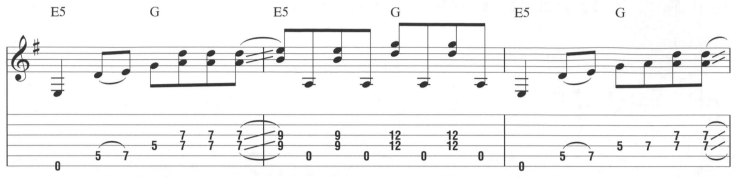

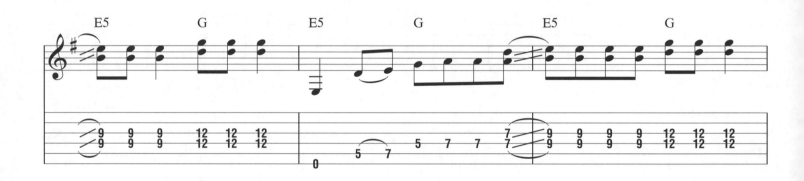

*D.C. al Coda*
*(no repeats)*

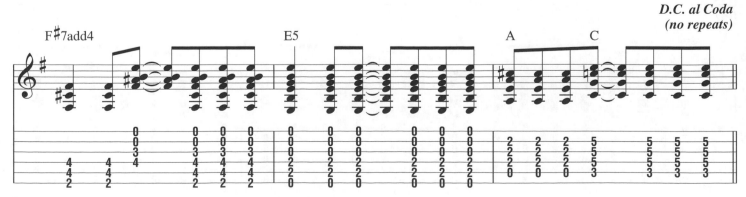

## ⊕ Coda

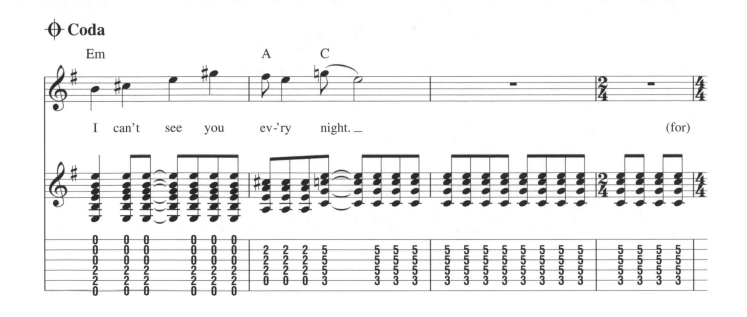

I can't see you ev'ry night. _ (for)

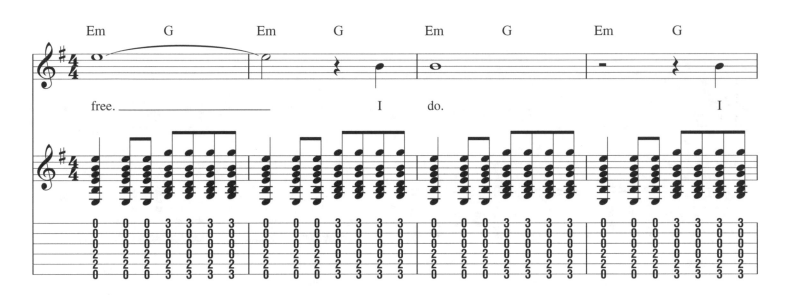

free. _____ I do. I

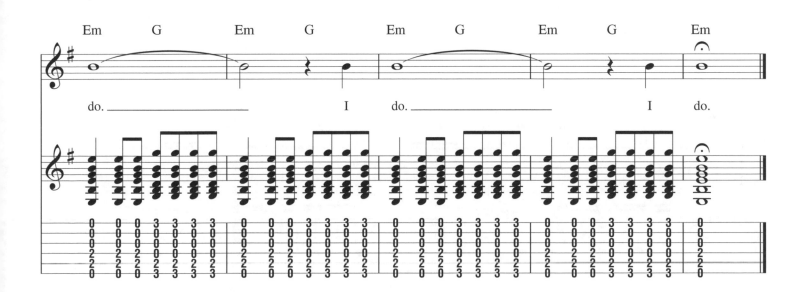

do. _____ I do. _____ I do.

*Additional Lyrics*

2. I'm standing in your line,
   I do, hope you have the time.
   I do, pick a number to,
   I do, keep a date with you.

# I'm Yours

**Words and Music by Jason Mraz**

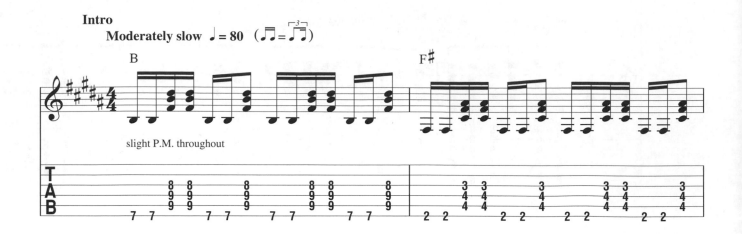

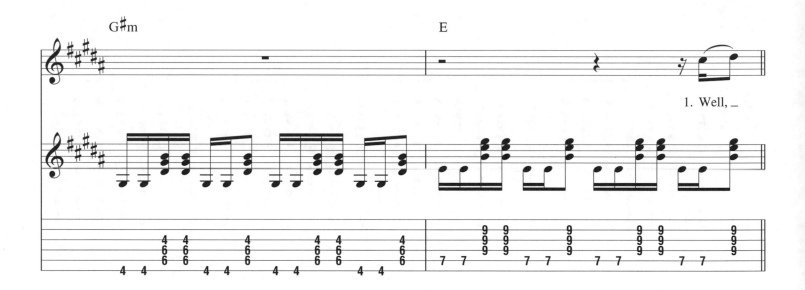

1. Well, _

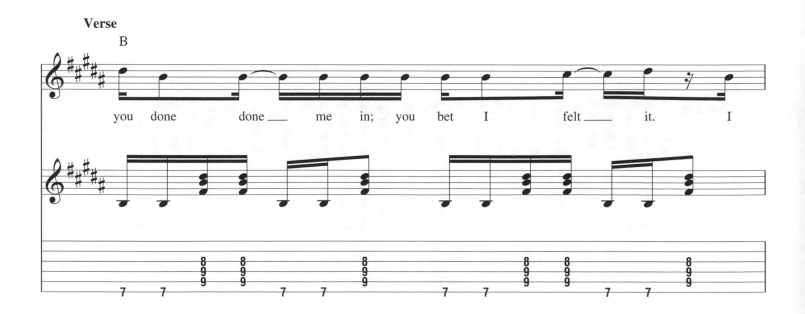

you done done __ me in; you bet I felt __ it. I

F#

tried to be chill, ___ but you're so hot that I melt - ed. I

G#m

fell right through the cracks. _____ Now I'm

E

try - ing to get ___ back. _____ Be - fore the

B

cool done run out, I'll be giv - ing it my best - est, and

**Verse**

2. Well, o - pen up your mind and see ___ like me. ___

O - pen up your plans and, damn, ___ you're free. ___

**Chorus**

**Interlude**

Skooch on o - ver clos - er, dear, and I will nib - ble your ear. _____ *Scat sing...*

3. I've been spend - ing

**Verse**

need to com-pli-cate 'cause our time is short. This is, this is, this is our

fate. I'm yours. _____ *Scat sing...*

**Outro**

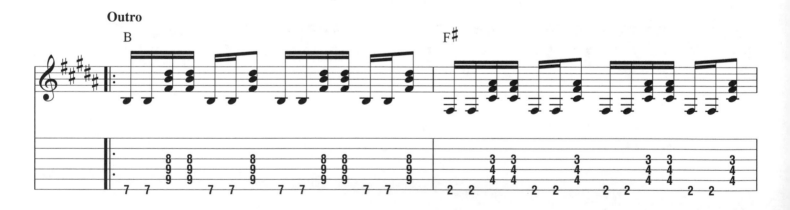

*Repeat and fade*

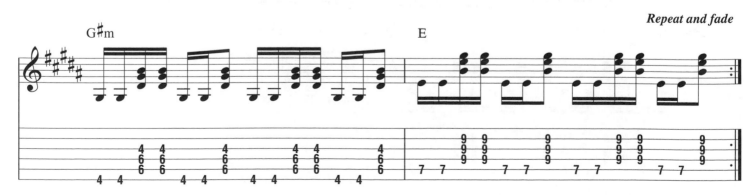

20

# The Scientist

**Words and Music by Guy Berryman, Jon Buckland, Will Champion and Chris Martin**

*To match original recording, place capo at 1st fret.

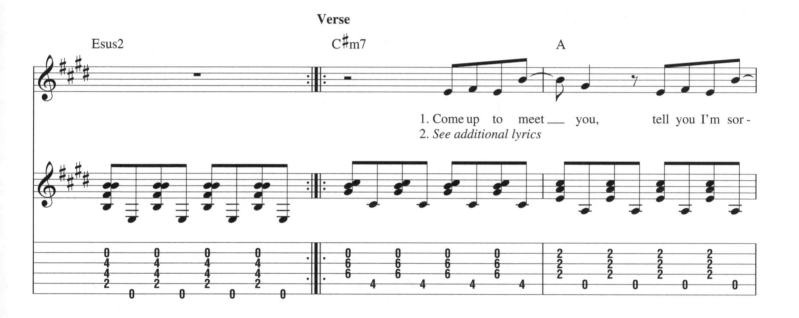

1. Come up to meet ___ you, tell you I'm sor-
2. *See additional lyrics*

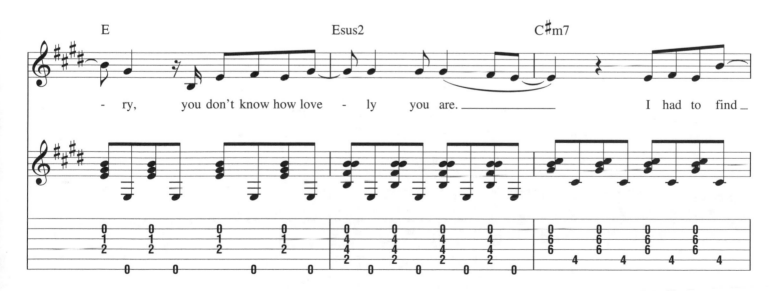

-ry, you don't know how love - ly you are. ___ I had to find ___

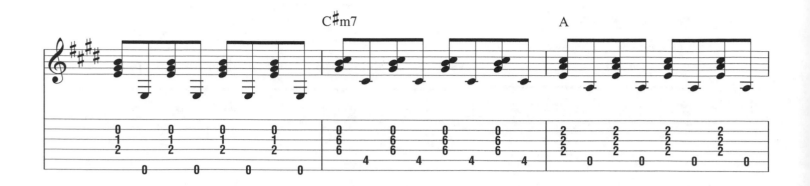

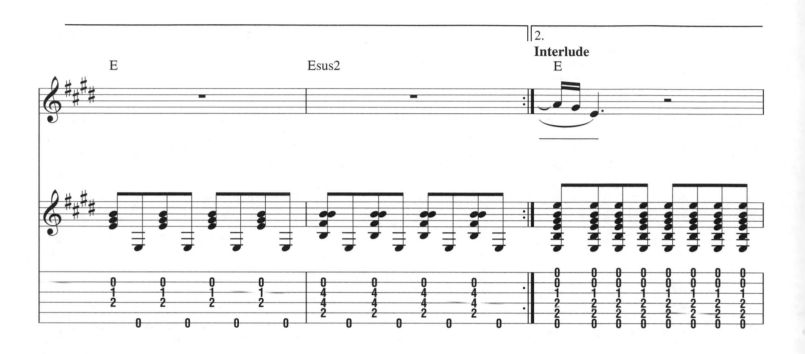

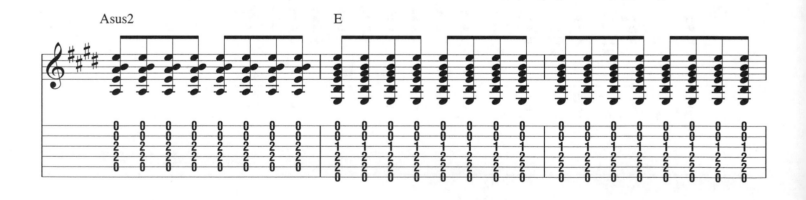

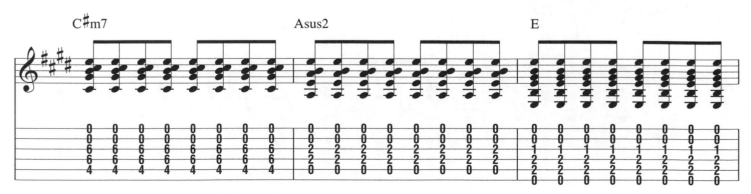

**Outro**

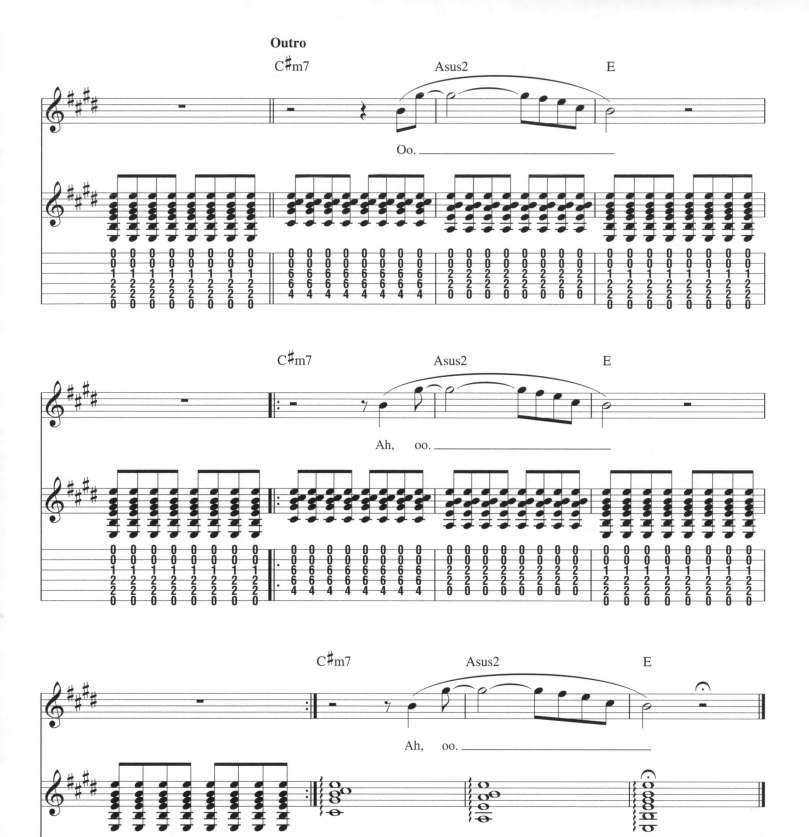

Oo.

Ah, oo.

Ah, oo.

*Additional Lyrics*

2. I was just guessin' at numbers and figures,
   Pullin' your puzzles apart.
   Questions of science, science and progress
   That must speak as loud as my heart.
   Tell me you love me, come back and haunt me.
   Oh, and I rush to the start.
   Runnin' in circles, chasing our tails.
   Comin' back as we are.

# The Lazy Song

**Words and Music by Bruno Mars, Ari Levine, Philip Lawrence and Keinan Warsame**

**Intro**

**Moderately** ♩ = 88

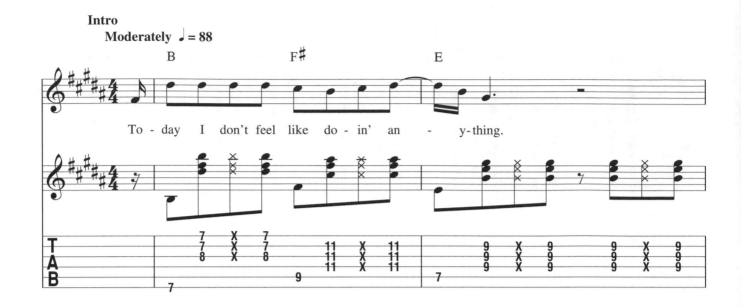

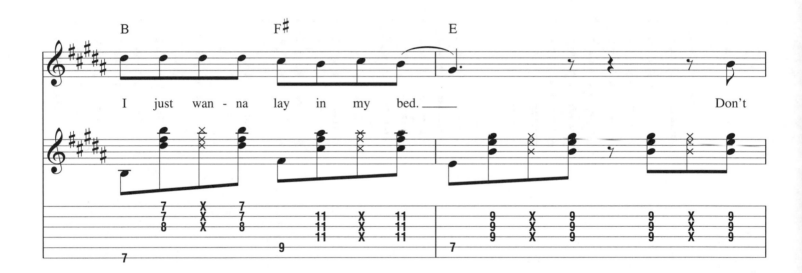

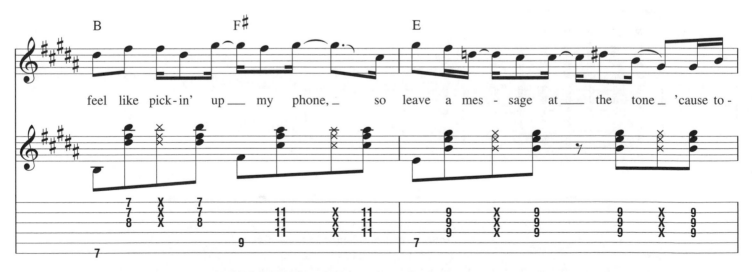

click to M - T - V so they can teach me how to doug - ie. 'Cause

B        F#        E

in my cas - tle, I'm the frick - in' _____ man. ___      Oh, ____

**Pre-Chorus**

C#m        D#m        E        F#

yes, I said it,     I said it.     I said it 'cause _ I can. _____     To -

𝄋 **Chorus**

B        F#        E

day I don't feel like do - in' an - y - thing.

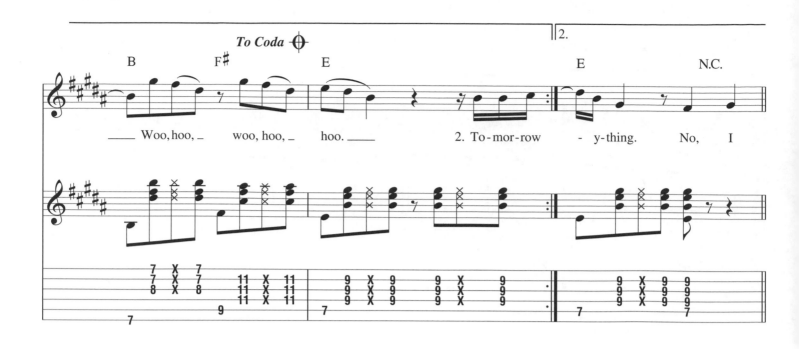

Woo, hoo, _ woo, hoo, _ hoo. _ 2. To-mor-row - y-thing. No, I

**Bridge**

ain't gon-na comb my hair 'cause I ain't go-in' an - y-where,

no, no, no, no, no, no, no, _ no, no, oh. I'll just

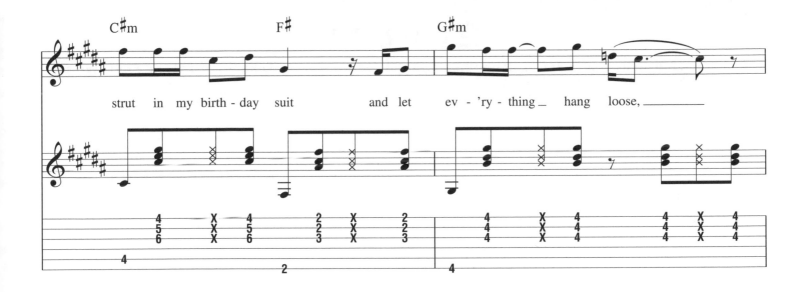

strut in my birth-day suit      and let ev-'ry-thing _ hang loose, _____

*D.S. al Coda*
*(take 1st ending)*

yeah, yeah, yeah, yeah, yeah, yeah, yeah, _ yeah, yeah,      yeah. _      Oh, _____ to-

⊕ **Coda**

hoo. _____      Noth-in' at      all. _____

*Additional Lyrics*

2. Tomorrow I'll wake up, do some P90X,
   Meet a really nice girl, have some really nice sex,
   And she's gonna scream out, "This is great."
   *Female (spoken):* (*Oh, my god, this is great.*)
   Yeah, I might mess around and get my college degree.
   I bet my old man will be so proud of me.
   Well, sorry, Pops, you'll just have to wait.

# 21 Guns

**Words and Music by David Bowie, John Phillips, Billie Joe Armstrong, Mike Pritchard and Frank Wright**

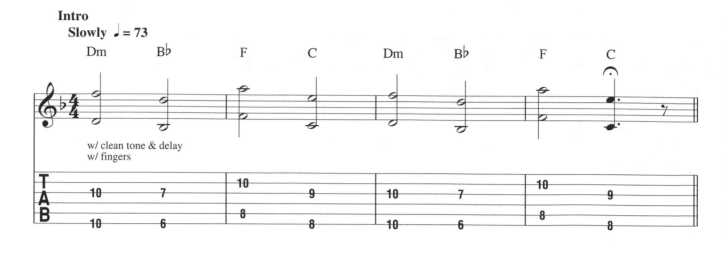

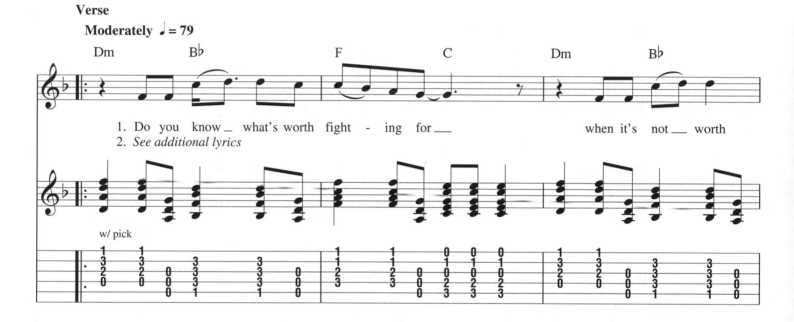

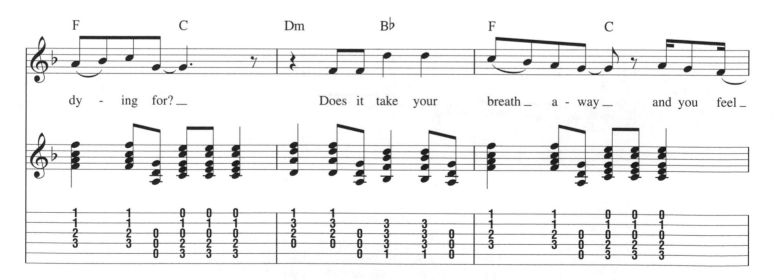

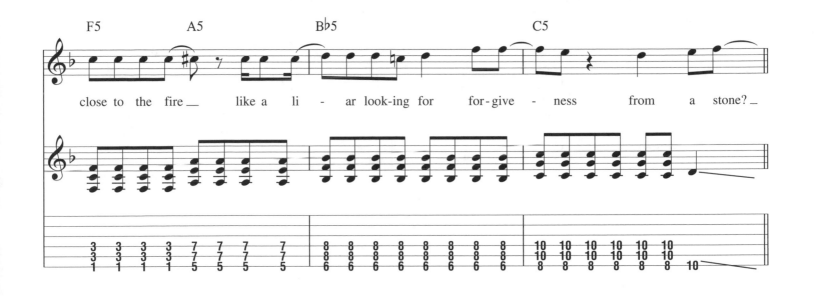

close to the fire __ like a li - ar look-ing for for-give - ness from a stone? __

**Interlude**

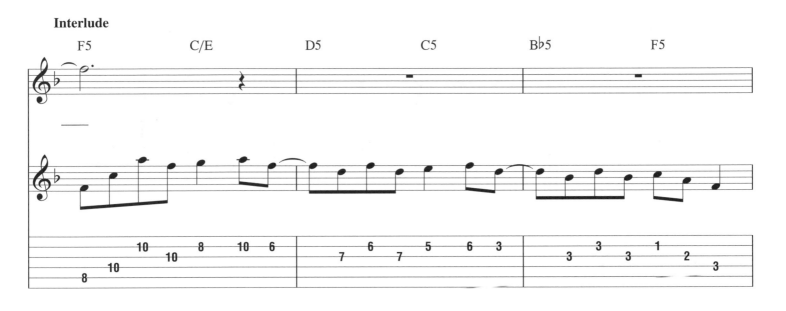

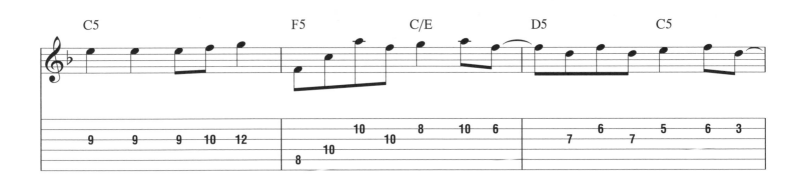

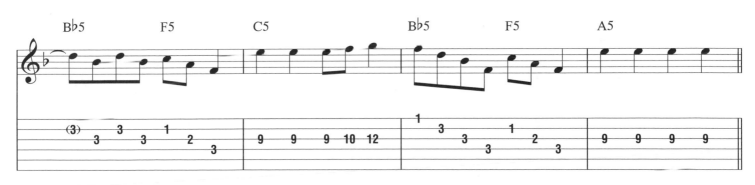

**Interlude**

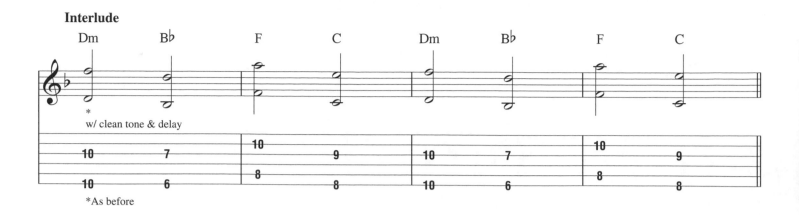

*
w/ clean tone & delay

*As before

3. When it's time ___ to ___ live and let die ___

w/ pick

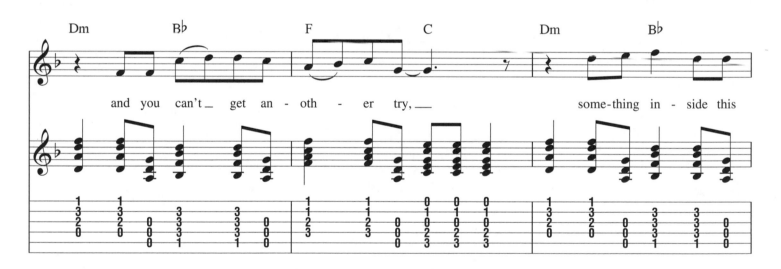

and you can't ___ get an - oth - er try, ___ some-thing in - side this

*D.S. al Coda*

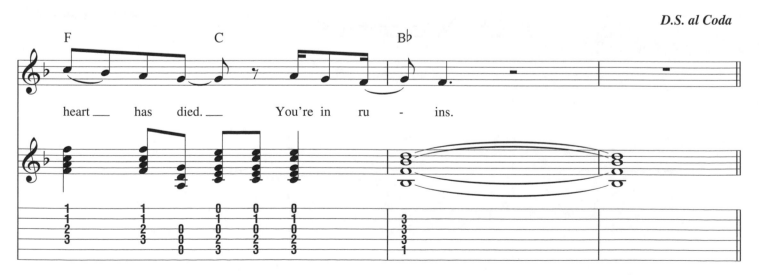

heart ___ has died. ___ You're in ru - ins.

## Coda

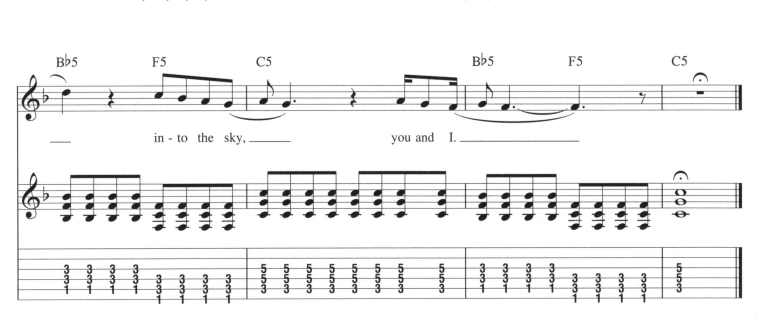

*Additional Lyrics*

2. When you're at the end of the road
   And you lost all sense of control.
   And your thoughts have taken their toll
   When your mind breaks the spirit of your soul.
   Your faith walks on broken glass
   And the hangover doesn't pass.
   Nothing's ever built to last.
   You're in ruins.

# What I Got

**Words and Music by Brad Nowell, Eric Wilson, Floyd Gaugh and Lindon Roberts**

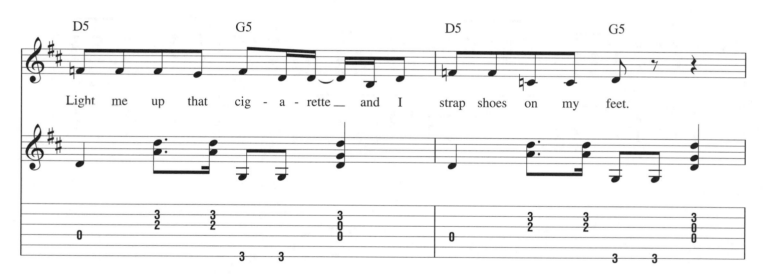

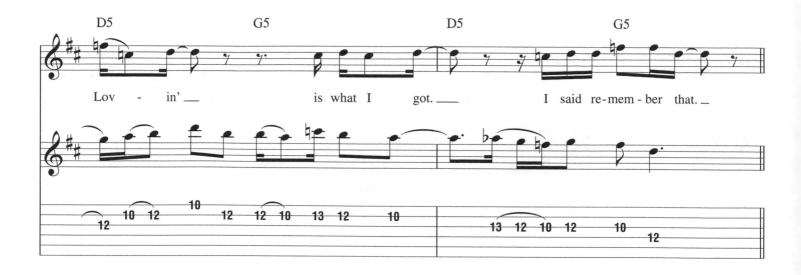

Lov - in' __ is what I got. __ I said re-mem-ber that. __

**Interlude**

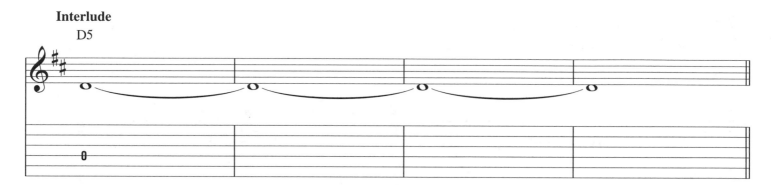

**Verse**

3. Why, I don't cry __ when my dog runs __ a-way. I don't get an-gry at the bills I have __ to pay.

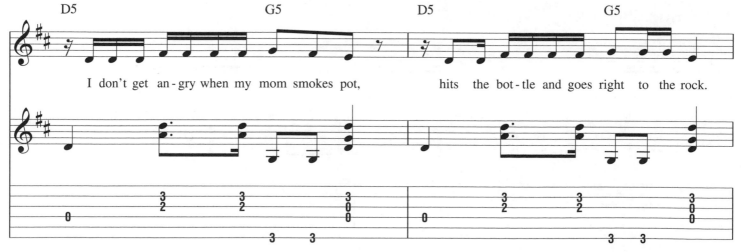

I don't get an-gry when my mom smokes pot, hits the bot-tle and goes right to the rock.

**Outro**

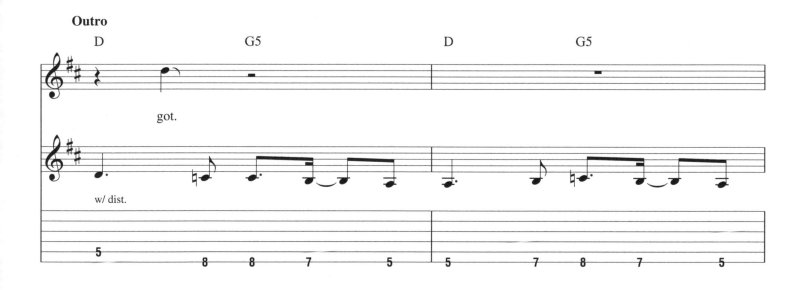

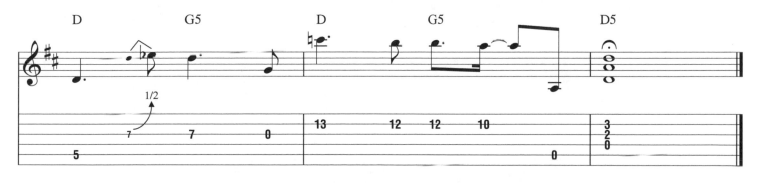

# Upside Down

from the Universal Pictures and Imagine Entertainment film CURIOUS GEORGE

**Words and Music by Jack Johnson**

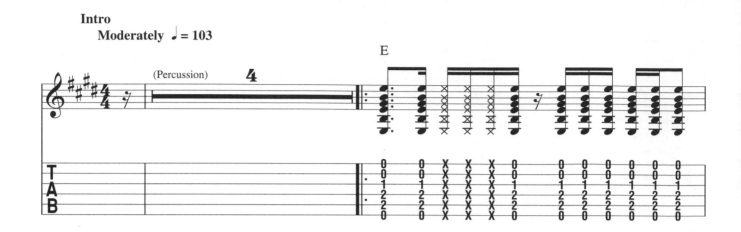

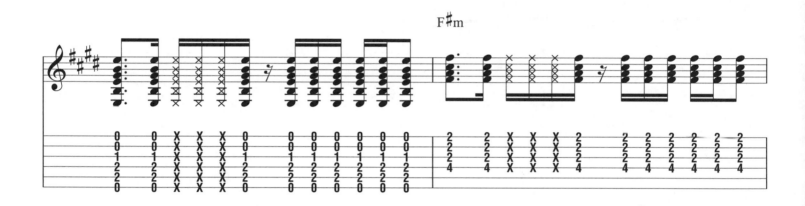

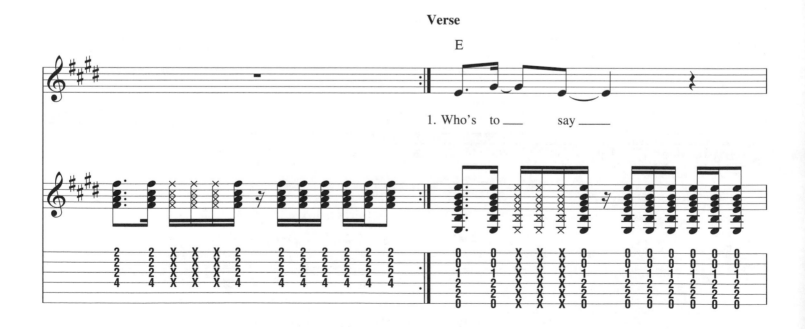

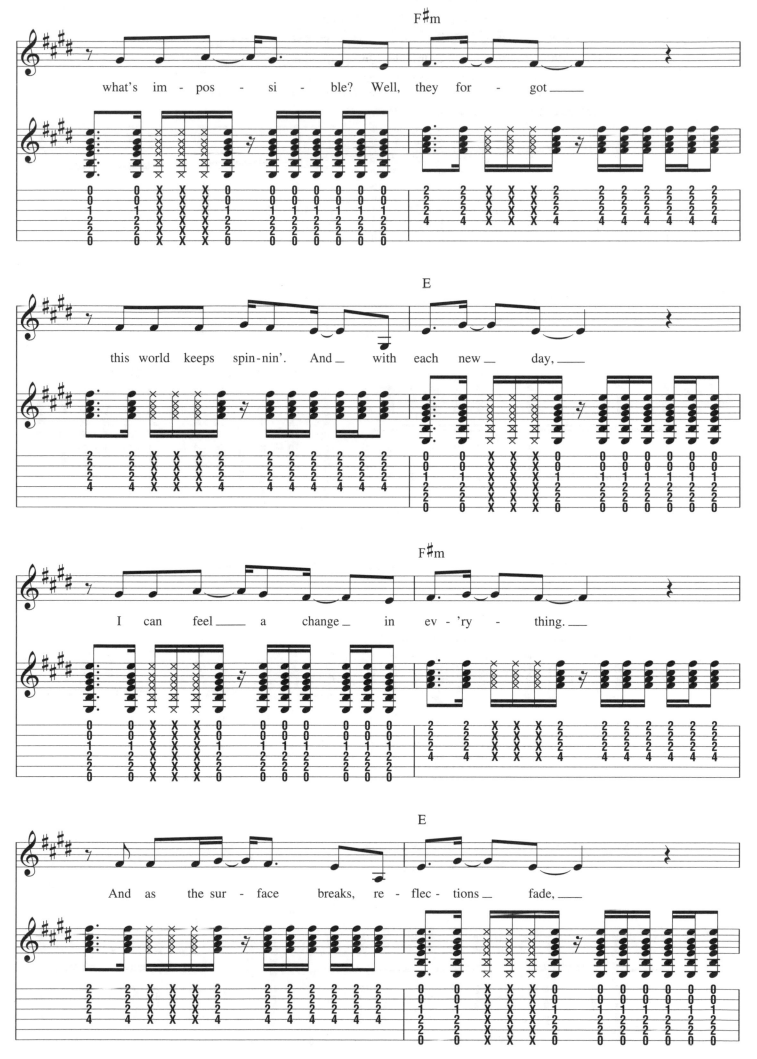

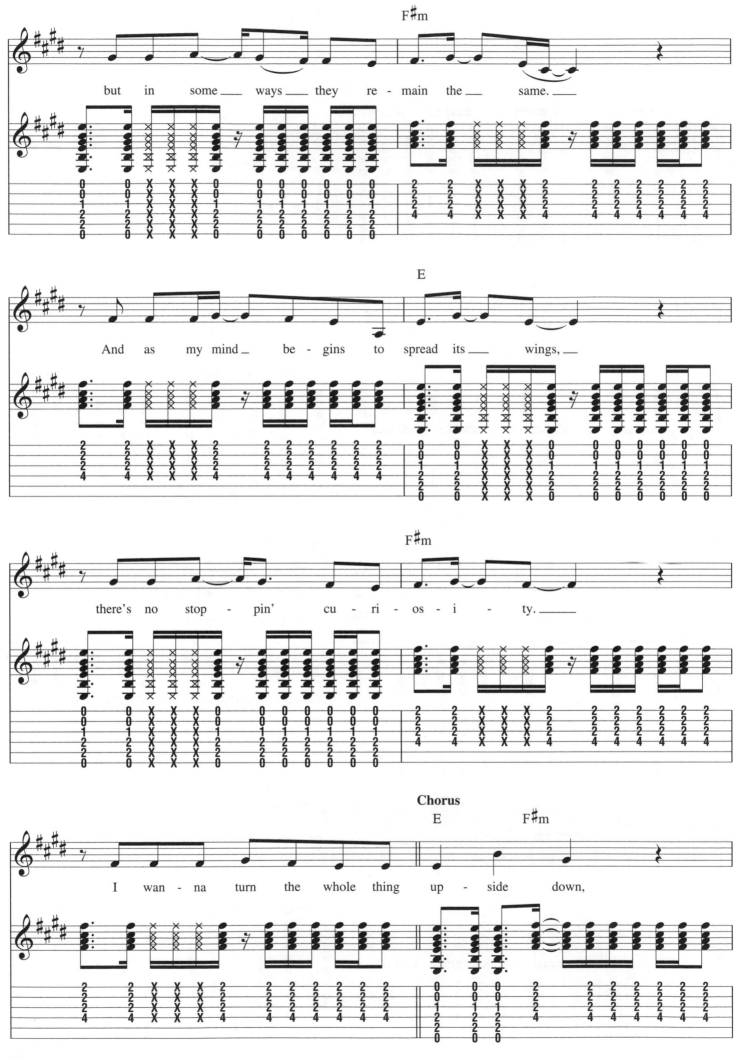

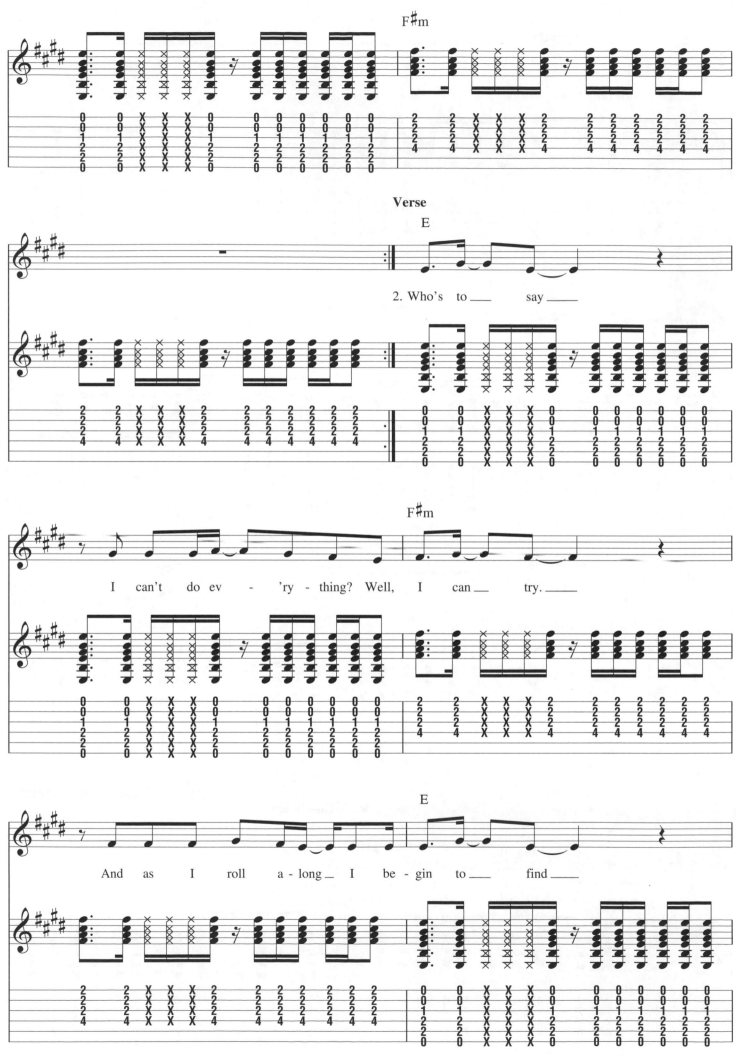

**Verse**

2. Who's to \_\_\_\_ say \_\_\_\_

I can't do ev - 'ry - thing? Well, I can \_\_\_\_ try. \_\_\_\_

And as I roll a - long \_\_\_\_ I be - gin to \_\_\_\_ find \_\_\_\_

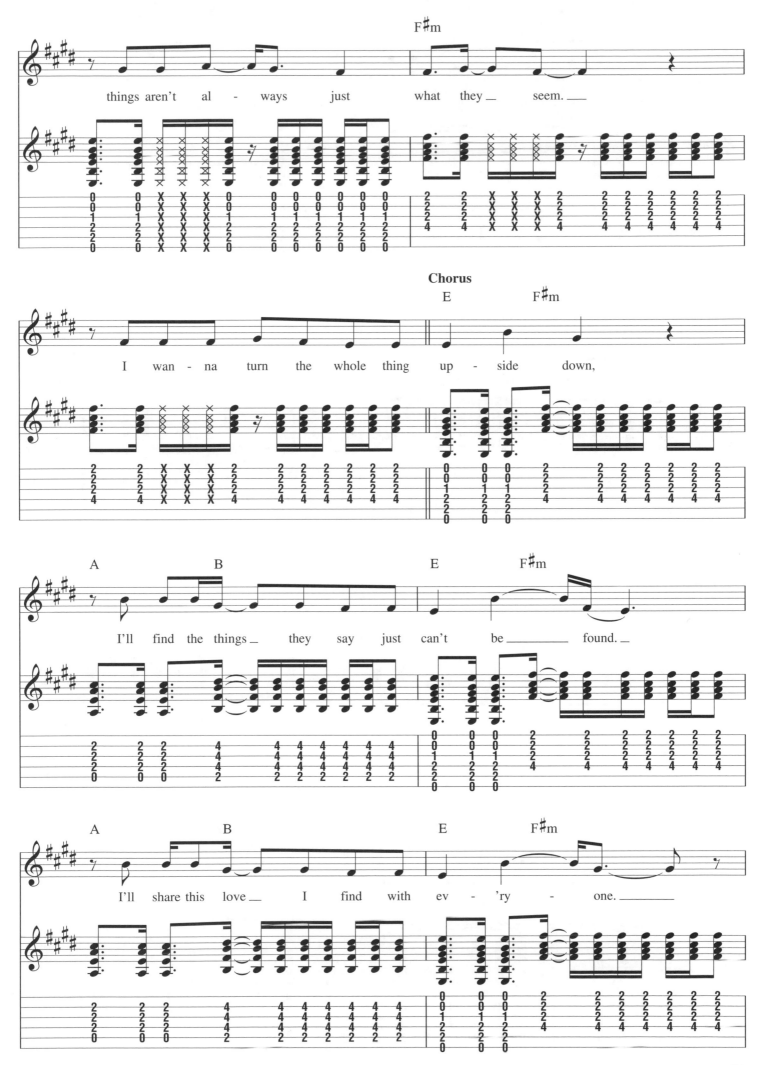

Who's to say what's im - pos - si - ble ___ and ___ can't be ___ found? ___

**Outro**

I don't want this feel - in' to go a - way. ___

Please ___ don't go a - way. ___

Please _ don't go a - way. _____

Please _ don't go a - way. _____

**Slower** ♩ = 84

Is this how it's sup-posed to be? _____

Is this how it's sup-posed to be? _____

54

# Wonderwall

**Words and Music by Noel Gallagher**

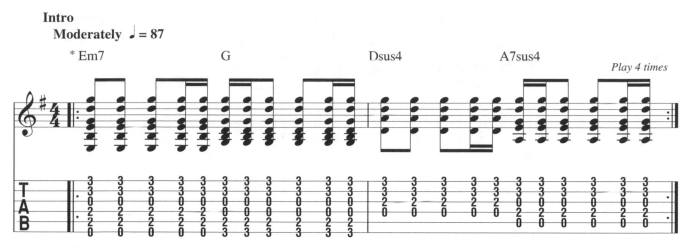

*To match original recording, place capo at 2nd fret.

**Verse**

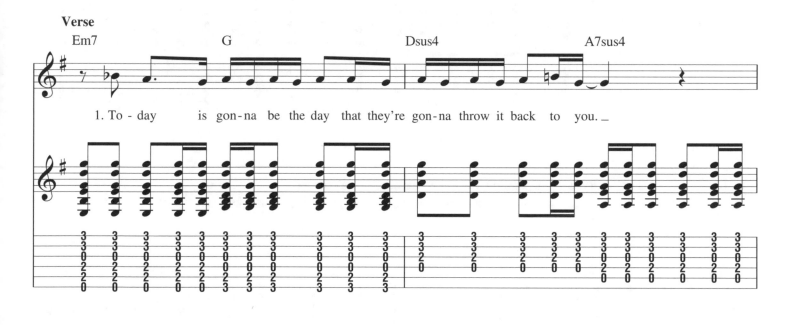

1. To-day      is gon-na be the day  that they're gon-na throw it back  to  you. __

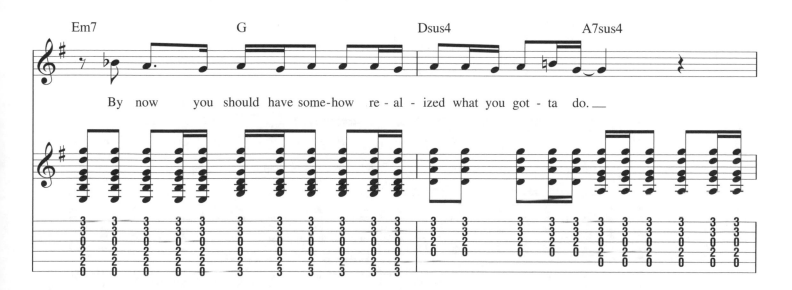

By  now      you  should have some-how  re-al-ized  what you got-ta  do. __

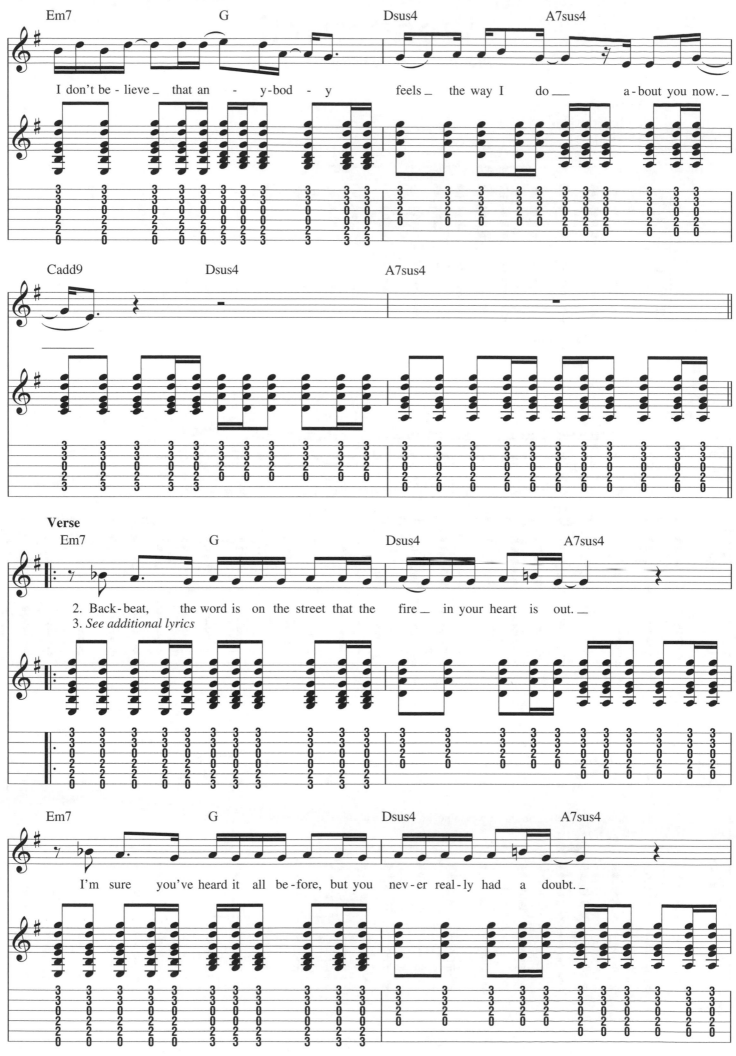

I don't be-lieve _ that an - - y-bod - y feels _ the way I do _ a-bout you now. _

Back-beat, the word is on the street that the fire _ in your heart is out.
3. *See additional lyrics*

I'm sure you've heard it all be-fore, but you nev-er real-ly had a doubt. _

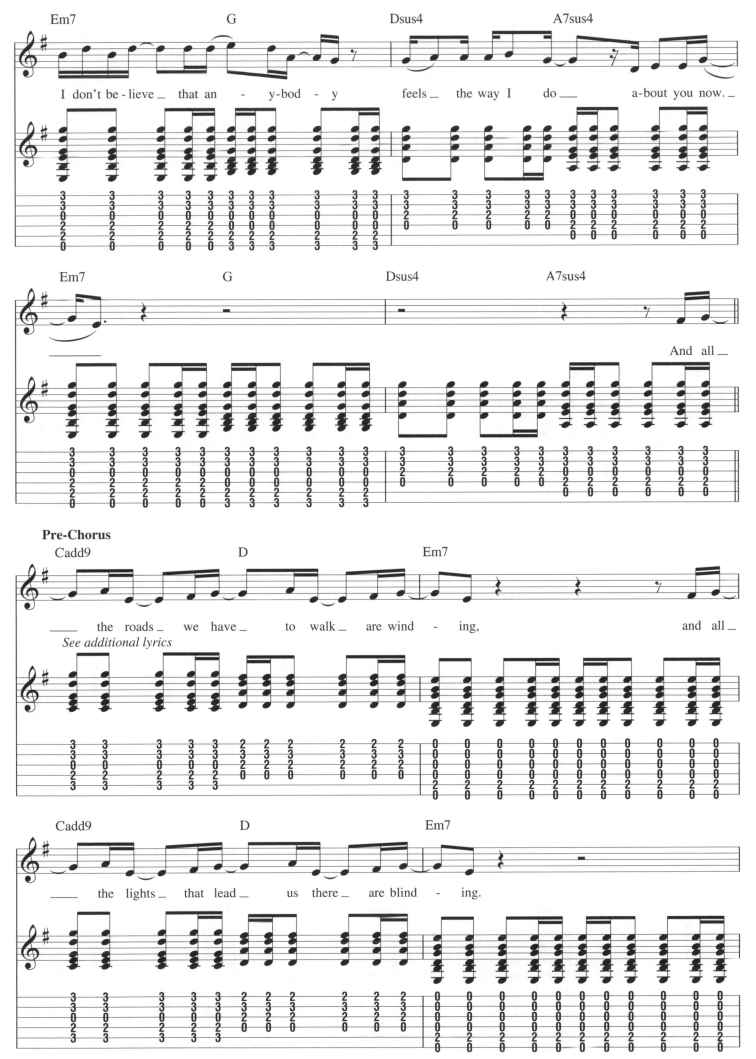

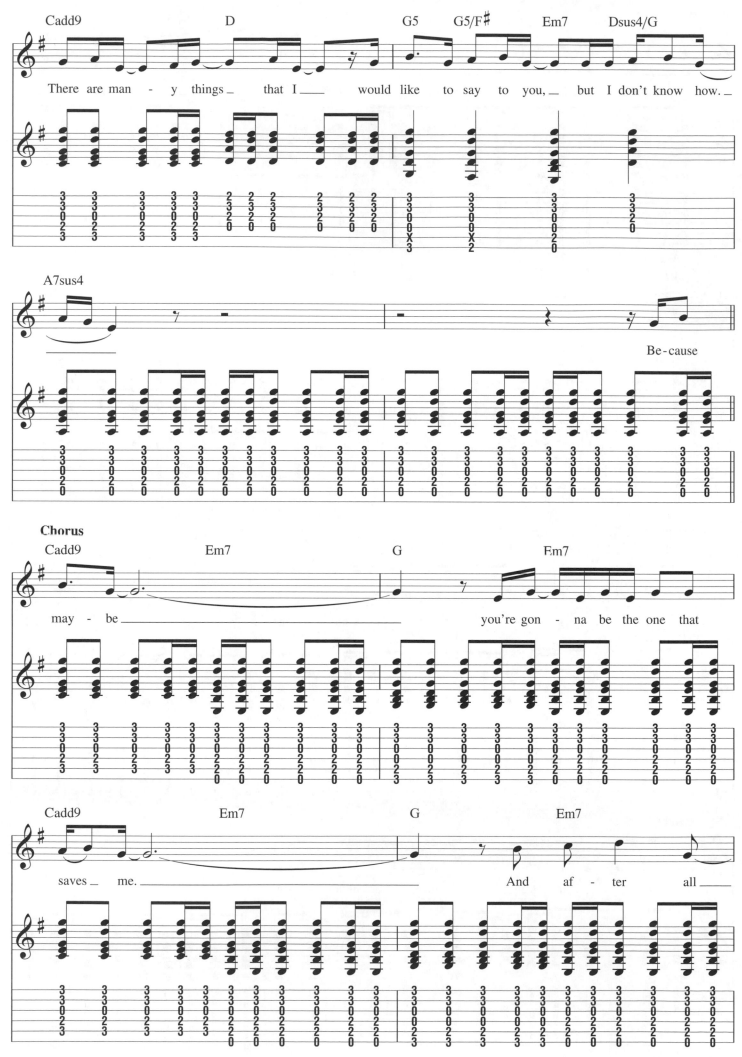

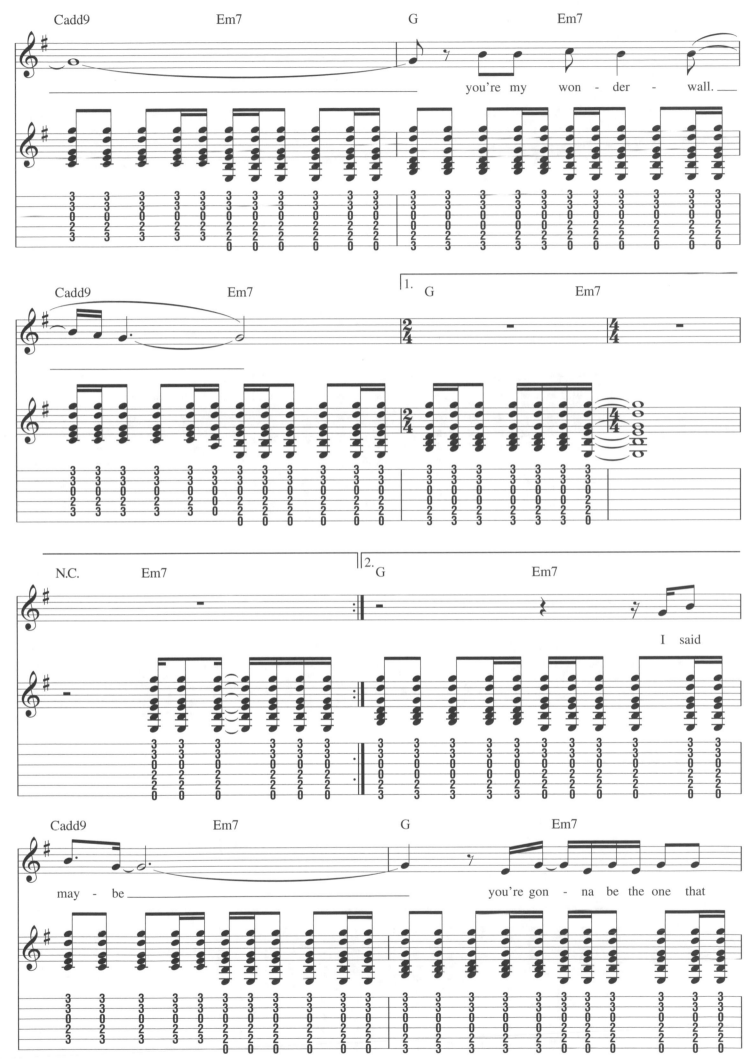

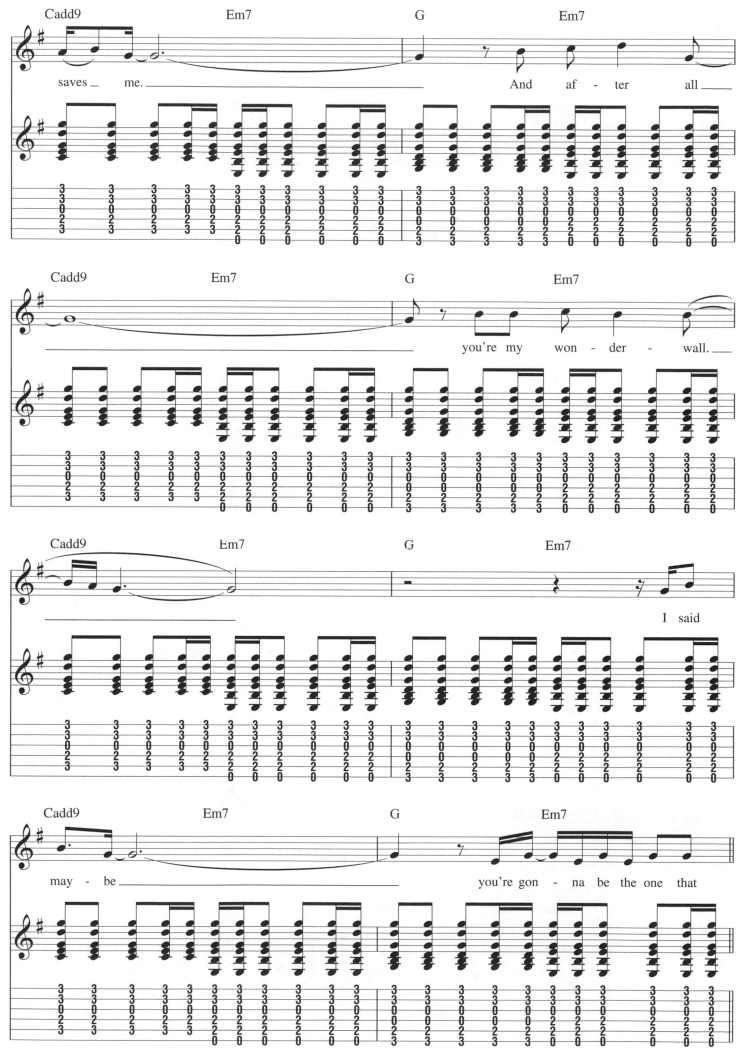

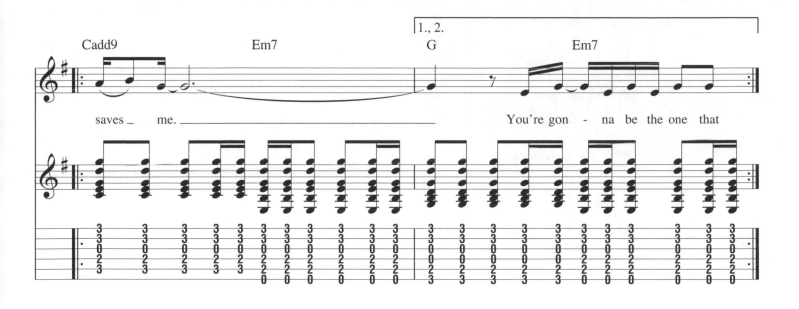

saves _ me. _____ You're gon - na be the one that

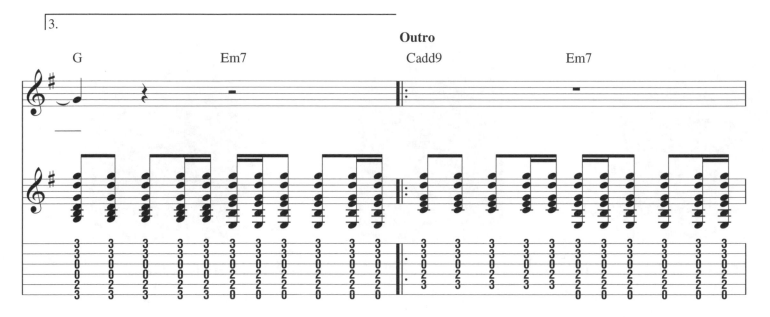

**Outro**

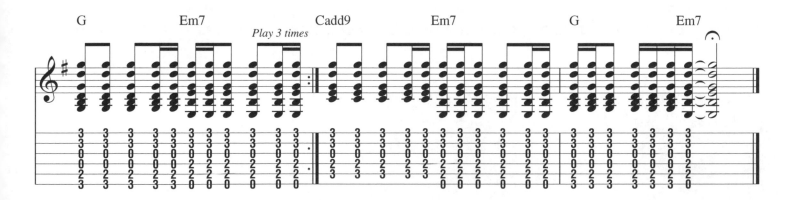

*Play 3 times*

*Additional Lyrics*

3. Today was gonna be the day, but they'll never throw it back to you.
By now you should have somehow realized what you're not to do.
I don't believe that anybody feels the way I do about you now.

*Pre-Chorus* 3. And all the roads that lead you there were winding,
And all the lights that light the way are blinding.
There are many things that I would like to say to you,
But I don't know how.
I said...

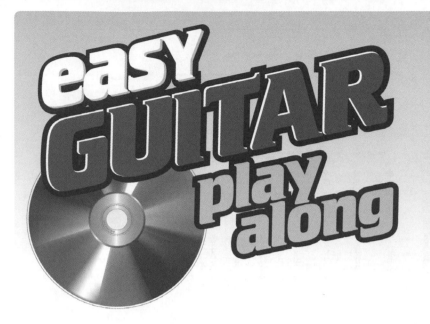

# easy GUITAR play along

The **easy GUITAR play along**® Series features streamlined transcriptions of your favorite songs. Just follow the tab, listen to the CD to hear how the guitar should sound, and then play along using the backing tracks. The CD is playable on any CD player, and is also enhanced to include the Amazing Slowdowner technology so Mac and PC users can adjust the recording to any tempo without changing the pitch!

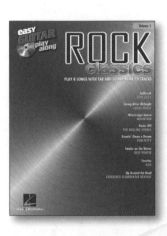

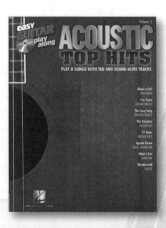

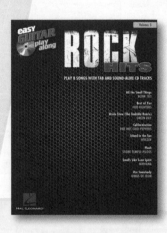

### 1. ROCK CLASSICS

Jailbreak • Living After Midnight • Mississippi Queen • Rocks Off • Runnin' Down a Dream • Smoke on the Water • Strutter • Up Around the Bend.

00702560 Book/CD Pack....$14.99

### 2. ACOUSTIC TOP HITS

About a Girl • I'm Yours • The Lazy Song • The Scientist • 21 Guns • Upside Down • What I Got • Wonderwall.

00702569 Book/CD Pack....$14.99

### 3. ROCK HITS

All the Small Things • Best of You • Brain Stew (The Godzilla Remix) • Californication • Island in the Sun • Plush • Smells like Teen Spirit • Use Somebody.

00702570 Book/CD Pack....$14.99

### 4. ROCK 'N' ROLL

Blue Suede Shoes • I Get Around • I'm a Believer • Jailhouse Rock • Oh, Pretty Woman • Peggy Sue • Runaway • Wake up Little Susie.

00702572 Book/CD Pack.....$14.99

### 5. ULTIMATE ACOUSTIC

Against the Wind • Babe, I'm Gonna Leave You • Come Monday • Free Fallin' • Give a Little Bit • Have You Ever Seen the Rain? • New Kid in Town • We Can Work It Out.

00702573 Book/CD Pack.....$14.99

**HAL•LEONARD®**
CORPORATION
7777 W. BLUEMOUND RD. P.O. BOX 13819
MILWAUKEE, WISCONSIN 53213

**www.halleonard.com**

Prices, contents, and availability subject to change without notice.

1211

# EASY GUITAR WITH NOTES & TAB

*This series features simplified arrangements with notes, tab, chord charts, and strum and pick patterns.*

## MIXED FOLIOS

| | | |
|---|---|---|
| 00702287 | Acoustic | $14.99 |
| 00702002 | Acoustic Rock Hits for Easy Guitar | $12.95 |
| 00702166 | All-Time Best Guitar Collection | $19.99 |
| 00699665 | Beatles Best | $12.95 |
| 00702232 | Best Acoustic Songs for Easy Guitar | $12.99 |
| 00702233 | Best Hard Rock Songs | $14.99 |
| 00698978 | Big Christmas Collection | $16.95 |
| 00702115 | Blues Classics | $10.95 |
| 00385020 | Broadway Songs for Kids | $9.95 |
| 00702237 | Christian Acoustic Favorites | $12.95 |
| 00702149 | Children's Christian Songbook | $7.95 |
| 00702028 | Christmas Classics | $7.95 |
| 00702185 | Christmas Hits | $9.95 |
| 00702016 | Classic Blues for Easy Guitar | $12.95 |
| 00702141 | Classic Rock | $8.95 |
| 00702203 | CMT's 100 Greatest Country Songs | $27.95 |
| 00702283 | The Contemporary Christian Collection | $16.99 |
| 00702006 | Contemporary Christian Favorites | $9.95 |
| 00702065 | Contemporary Women of Country | $9.95 |
| 00702239 | Country Classics for Easy Guitar | $19.99 |
| 00702295 | Country Hits of 2010-2011 | $14.99 |
| 00702282 | Country Hits of 2009-2010 | $14.99 |
| 00702240 | Country Hits of 2007-2008 | $12.95 |
| 00702225 | Country Hits of '06-'07 | $12.95 |
| 00702085 | Disney Movie Hits | $12.95 |
| 00702257 | Easy Acoustic Guitar Songs | $14.99 |
| 00702280 | Easy Guitar Tab White Pages | $29.99 |
| 00702212 | Essential Christmas | $9.95 |
| 00702041 | Favorite Hymns for Easy Guitar | $9.95 |

| | | |
|---|---|---|
| 00702281 | 4 Chord Rock | $9.99 |
| 00702286 | Glee | $16.99 |
| 00702174 | God Bless America® & Other Songs for a Better Nation | $8.95 |
| 00699374 | Gospel Favorites | $14.95 |
| 00702160 | The Great American Country Songbook | $14.95 |
| 00702050 | Great Classical Themes for Easy Guitar | $6.95 |
| 00702131 | Great Country Hits of the '90s | $8.95 |
| 00702116 | Greatest Hymns for Guitar | $8.95 |
| 00702130 | The Groovy Years | $9.95 |
| 00702184 | Guitar Instrumentals | $9.95 |
| 00702231 | High School Musical for Easy Guitar | $12.95 |
| 00702241 | High School Musical 2 | $12.95 |
| 00702046 | Hits of the '70s for Easy Guitar | $8.95 |
| 00702032 | International Songs for Easy Guitar | $12.95 |
| 00702273 | Irish Songs | $12.99 |
| 00702275 | Jazz Favorites for Easy Guitar | $14.99 |
| 00702274 | Jazz Standards for Easy Guitar | $14.99 |
| 00702051 | Jock Rock for Easy Guitar | $9.95 |
| 00702162 | Jumbo Easy Guitar Songbook | $19.95 |
| 00702112 | Latin Favorites | $9.95 |
| 00702258 | Legends of Rock | $14.99 |
| 00702138 | Mellow Rock Hits | $10.95 |
| 00702261 | Modern Worship Hits | $14.99 |
| 00702147 | Motown's Greatest Hits | $9.95 |
| 00702189 | MTV's 100 Greatest Pop Songs | $24.95 |
| 00702272 | 1950s Rock | $14.99 |
| 00702271 | 1960s Rock | $14.99 |
| 00702270 | 1970s Rock | $14.99 |

| | | |
|---|---|---|
| 00702269 | 1980s Rock | $14.99 |
| 00702268 | 1990s Rock | $14.99 |
| 00702187 | Selections from O Brother Where Art Thou? | $12.95 |
| 00702178 | 100 Songs for Kids | $12.95 |
| 00702515 | Pirates of the Caribbean | $12.99 |
| 00702125 | Praise and Worship for Guitar | $9.95 |
| 00702155 | Rock Hits for Guitar | $9.95 |
| 00702242 | Rock Band | $19.95 |
| 00702256 | Rock Band 2 | $19.99 |
| 00702128 | Rockin' Down the Highway | $9.95 |
| 00702110 | The Sound of Music | $9.99 |
| 00702285 | Southern Rock Hits | $12.99 |
| 00702124 | Today's Christian Rock – 2nd Edition | $9.95 |
| 00702220 | Today's Country Hits | $9.95 |
| 00702198 | Today's Hits for Guitar | $9.95 |
| 00702217 | Top Christian Hits | $12.95 |
| 00702235 | Top Christian Hits of '07-'08 | $14.95 |
| 00702556 | Top Hits of 2011 | $14.99 |
| 00702284 | Top Hits of 2010 | $14.99 |
| 00702246 | Top Hits of 2008 | $12.95 |
| 00702294 | Top Worship Hits | $14.99 |
| 00702206 | Very Best of Rock | $9.95 |
| 00702255 | VH1's 100 Greatest Hard Rock Songs | $27.99 |
| 00702175 | VH1's 100 Greatest Songs of Rock and Roll | $24.95 |
| 00702253 | Wicked | $12.99 |
| 00702192 | Worship Favorites | $9.95 |

## ARTIST COLLECTIONS

| | | |
|---|---|---|
| 00702267 | AC/DC for Easy Guitar | $14.99 |
| 00702598 | Adele for Easy Guitar | $12.99 |
| 00702001 | Best of Aerosmith | $16.95 |
| 00702040 | Best of the Allman Brothers | $14.99 |
| 00702169 | Best of The Beach Boys | $12.99 |
| 00702292 | The Beatles – 1 | $19.99 |
| 00702201 | The Essential Black Sabbath | $12.95 |
| 00702140 | Best of Brooks & Dunn | $10.95 |
| 02501615 | Zac Brown Band – The Foundation | $16.99 |
| 02501621 | Zac Brown Band – You Get What You Give | $16.99 |
| 00702095 | Best of Mariah Carey | $12.95 |
| 00702043 | Best of Johnny Cash | $14.99 |
| 00702033 | Best of Steven Curtis Chapman | $14.95 |
| 00702291 | Very Best of Coldplay | $12.99 |
| 00702263 | Best of Casting Crowns | $12.99 |
| 00702090 | Eric Clapton's Best | $10.95 |
| 00702086 | Eric Clapton – from the Album Unplugged | $10.95 |
| 00702202 | The Essential Eric Clapton | $12.95 |
| 00702250 | blink-182 – Greatest Hits | $12.99 |
| 00702053 | Best of Patsy Cline | $10.95 |
| 00702229 | The Very Best of Creedence Clearwater Revival | $12.95 |
| 00702145 | Best of Jim Croce | $10.95 |
| 00702278 | Crosby, Stills & Nash | $12.99 |
| 00702219 | David Crowder*Band Collection | $12.95 |
| 00702122 | The Doors for Easy Guitar | $12.99 |
| 00702276 | Fleetwood Mac – Easy Guitar Collection | $12.99 |
| 00702099 | Best of Amy Grant | $9.95 |
| 00702190 | Best of Pat Green | $19.95 |

| | | |
|---|---|---|
| 00702136 | Best of Merle Haggard | $12.99 |
| 00702243 | Hannah Montana | $14.95 |
| 00702244 | Hannah Montana 2/Meet Miley Cyrus | $16.95 |
| 00702227 | Jimi Hendrix – Smash Hits | $14.99 |
| 00702288 | Best of Hillsong United | $12.99 |
| 00702236 | Best of Antonio Carlos Jobim | $12.95 |
| 00702087 | Best of Billy Joel | $10.95 |
| 00702245 | Elton John – Greatest Hits 1970-2002 | $14.99 |
| 00702204 | Robert Johnson | $9.95 |
| 00702277 | Best of Jonas Brothers | $14.99 |
| 00702234 | Selections from Toby Keith – 35 Biggest Hits | $12.95 |
| 00702003 | Kiss | $9.95 |
| 00702193 | Best of Jennifer Knapp | $12.95 |
| 00702097 | John Lennon – Imagine | $9.95 |
| 00702216 | Lynyrd Skynyrd | $15.99 |
| 00702182 | The Essential Bob Marley | $12.95 |
| 00702346 | Bruno Mars – Doo-Wops & Hooligans | $12.99 |
| 00702248 | Paul McCartney – All the Best | $14.99 |
| 00702129 | Songs of Sarah McLachlan | $12.95 |
| 02501316 | Metallica – Death Magnetic | $15.95 |
| 00702209 | Steve Miller Band – Young Hearts (Greatest Hits) | $12.95 |
| 00702096 | Best of Nirvana | $14.95 |
| 00702211 | The Offspring – Greatest Hits | $12.95 |
| 00702030 | Best of Roy Orbison | $12.95 |
| 00702144 | Best of Ozzy Osbourne | $14.99 |
| 00702279 | Tom Petty | $12.99 |
| 00702139 | Elvis Country Favorites | $9.95 |
| 00702293 | The Very Best of Prince | $12.99 |
| 00699415 | Best of Queen for Guitar | $14.99 |

| | | |
|---|---|---|
| 00702208 | Red Hot Chili Peppers – Greatest Hits | $12.95 |
| 00702093 | Rolling Stones Collection | $17.95 |
| 00702092 | Best of the Rolling Stones | $14.99 |
| 00702196 | Best of Bob Seger | $12.95 |
| 00702252 | Frank Sinatra – Nothing But the Best | $12.99 |
| 00702010 | Best of Rod Stewart | $14.95 |
| 00702150 | Best of Sting | $12.95 |
| 00702049 | Best of George Strait | $12.95 |
| 00702259 | Taylor Swift for Easy Guitar | $12.99 |
| 00702290 | Taylor Swift – Speak Now | $14.99 |
| 00702223 | Chris Tomlin – Arriving | $12.95 |
| 00702262 | Chris Tomlin Collection | $14.99 |
| 00702226 | Chris Tomlin – See the Morning | $12.95 |
| 00702132 | Shania Twain – Greatest Hits | $10.95 |
| 00702108 | Best of Stevie Ray Vaughan | $10.95 |
| 00702123 | Best of Hank Williams | $12.99 |
| 00702111 | Stevie Wonder – Guitar Collection | $9.95 |
| 00702228 | Neil Young – Greatest Hits | $14.99 |
| 00702188 | Essential ZZ Top | $10.95 |

Prices, contents and availability subject to change without notice.

FOR MORE INFORMATION, SEE YOUR LOCAL MUSIC DEALER, OR WRITE TO:

HAL•LEONARD® CORPORATION

7777 W. BLUEMOUND RD. P.O. BOX 13819 MILWAUKEE, WI 53213

Visit Hal Leonard online at
**www.halleonard.com**

1211

# THE BOOK SERIES
## FOR EASY GUITAR

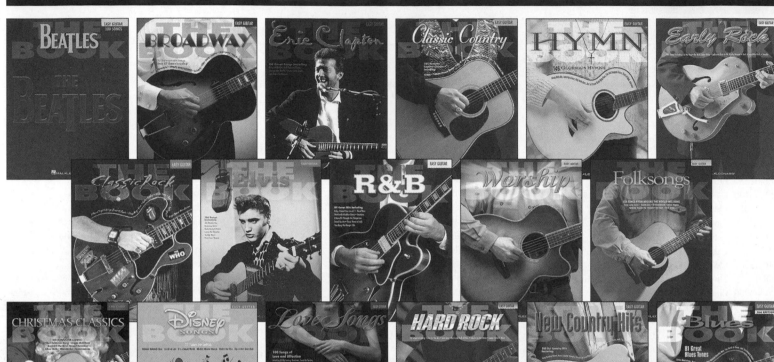

## THE ACOUSTIC BOOK
00702251 Easy Guitar ...................................$16.99

## THE BEATLES BOOK
00699266 Easy Guitar ...................................$19.95

## THE BLUES BOOK – 2ND ED.
00702104 Easy Guitar ...................................$16.95

## THE BROADWAY BOOK
00702015 Easy Guitar ...................................$17.95

## THE CHRISTMAS CAROLS BOOK
00702186 Easy Guitar ...................................$14.95

## THE CHRISTMAS CLASSICS BOOK
00702200 Easy Guitar ...................................$14.95

## THE ERIC CLAPTON BOOK
00702056 Easy Guitar ...................................$18.95

## THE CLASSIC COUNTRY BOOK
00702018 Easy Guitar ...................................$19.95

## THE CLASSIC ROCK BOOK
00698977 Easy Guitar ...................................$19.95

## THE CONTEMPORARY CHRISTIAN BOOK
00702195 Easy Guitar ...................................$16.95

## THE COUNTRY CLASSIC FAVORITES BOOK
00702238 Easy Guitar ...................................$19.99

## THE DISNEY SONGS BOOK
00702168 Easy Guitar ...................................$19.95

## THE FOLKSONGS BOOK
00702180 Easy Guitar ...................................$14.95

## THE GOSPEL SONGS BOOK
00702157 Easy Guitar ...................................$15.95

## THE HARD ROCK BOOK
00702181 Easy Guitar ...................................$16.95

## THE HYMN BOOK
00702142 Easy Guitar ...................................$14.99

## THE JAZZ STANDARDS BOOK
00702164 Easy Guitar ...................................$15.95

## THE LOVE SONGS BOOK
00702064 Easy Guitar ...................................$16.95

## THE NEW COUNTRY HITS BOOK
00702017 Easy Guitar ...................................$19.95

## THE ELVIS BOOK
00702163 Easy Guitar ...................................$19.95

## THE R&B BOOK
0702058 Easy Guitar ...................................$16.95

## THE ROCK CLASSICS BOOK
00702055 Easy Guitar ...................................$18.95

## THE WEDDING SONGS BOOK
00702167 Easy Guitar ...................................$16.95

## THE WORSHIP BOOK
00702247 Easy Guitar ...................................$14.99

**www.halleonard.com**

Prices, contents, and availability subject
to change without notice.

Disney characters and artwork © Disney Enterprises, Inc.

FOR MORE INFORMATION, SEE YOUR LOCAL MUSIC DEALER,
OR WRITE TO:

HAL•LEONARD®
CORPORATION

7777 W. BLUEMOUND RD. P.O. BOX 13819 MILWAUKEE, WI 53213

0811

ISBN 978-1-4950-6898-0

HAL•LEONARD®
CORPORATION
7777 W. BLUEMOUND RD. P.O. BOX 13819 MILWAUKEE, WI 53213

Visit Hal Leonard Online at
**www.halleonard.com**

# CONTENTS

# ALL I WANT FOR CHRISTMAS IS MY TWO FRONT TEETH

Words and Music by
DON GARDNER

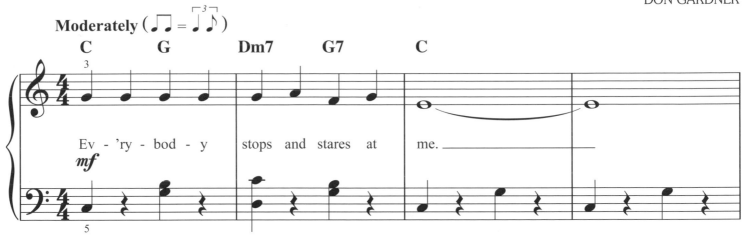

Moderately

Ev - 'ry - bod - y stops and stares at me. _____

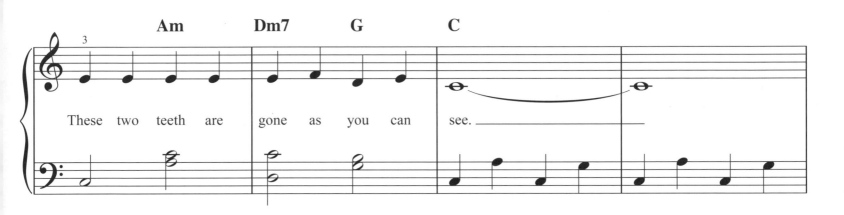

These two teeth are gone as you can see. _____

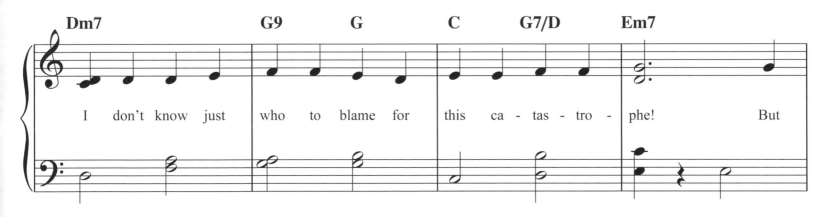

I don't know just who to blame for this ca - tas - tro - phe! But

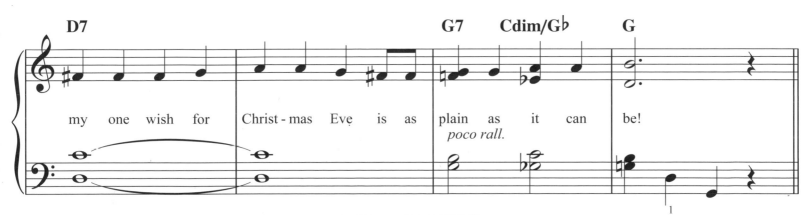

my one wish for Christ - mas Eve is as plain as it can be!
poco rall.

4

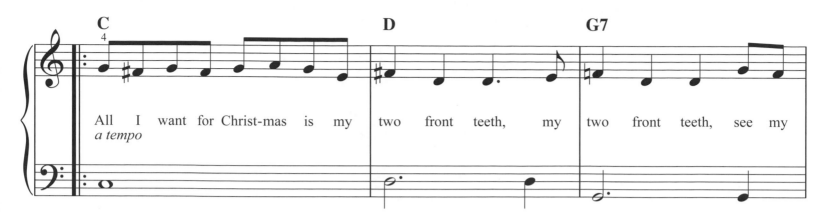

All I want for Christ-mas is my two front teeth, my two front teeth, see my
*a tempo*

two front teeth! Gee, if I could on - ly have my two front teeth, then

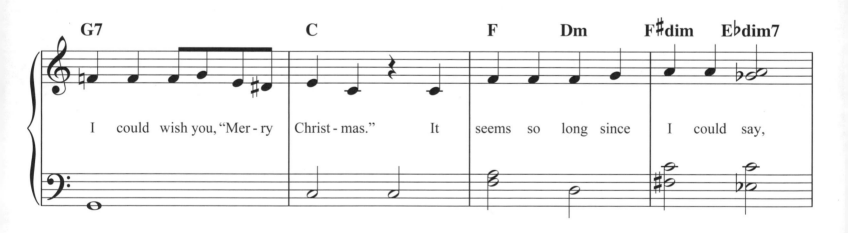

I could wish you, "Mer - ry Christ - mas." It seems so long since I could say,

"Sis - ter Su - sie sit - ting on a this - tle!" Gosh, oh gee, how hap - py I'd be, if

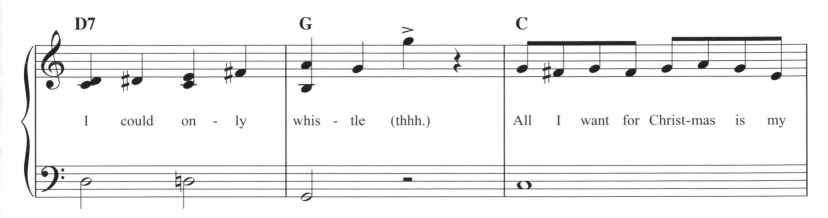

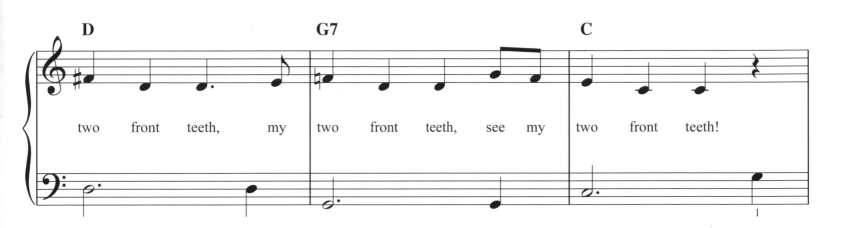

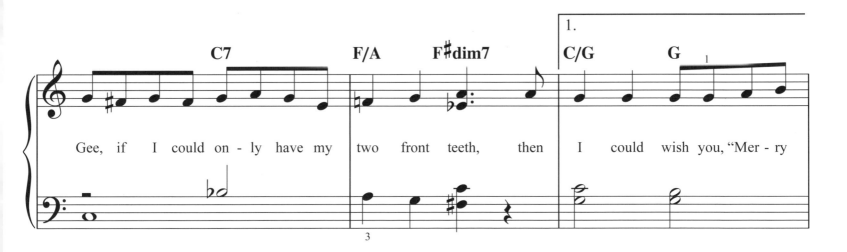

# All I WANT FOR CHRISTMAS IS YOU

Words and Music by MARIAH CAREY
and WALTER AFANASIEFF

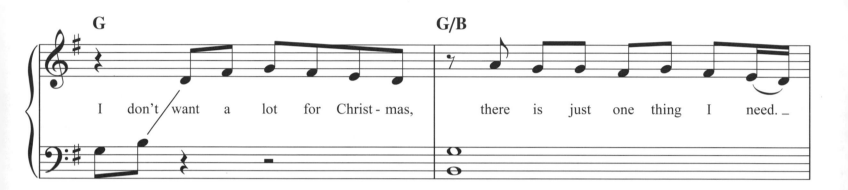

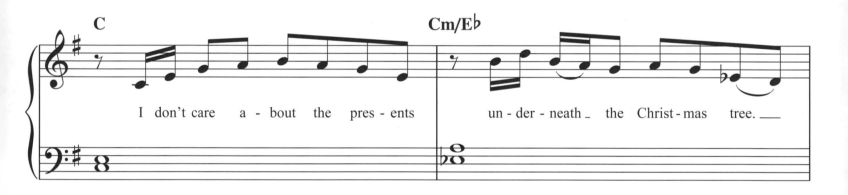

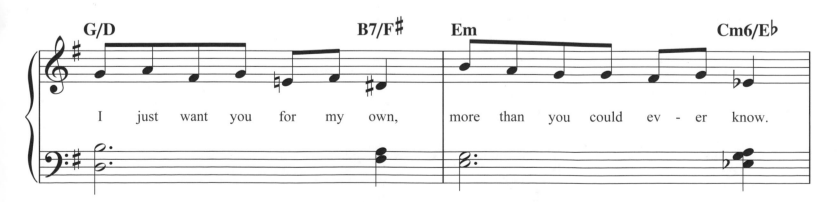

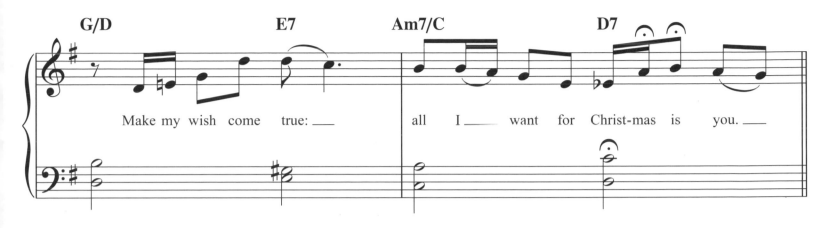

Make my wish come true: \_\_\_ all I \_\_\_ want for Christ-mas is you. \_\_\_

**Moderately** ( ♫ = ♩♪ )

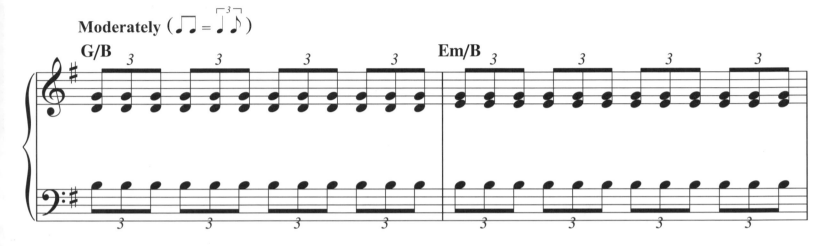

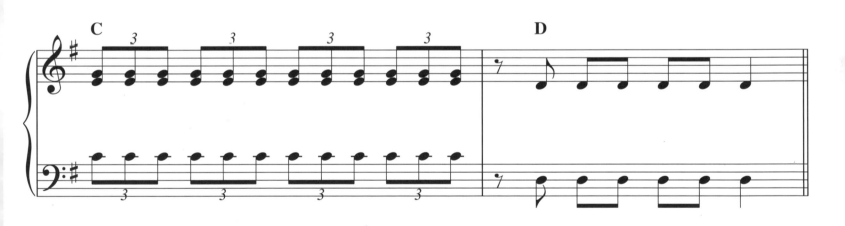

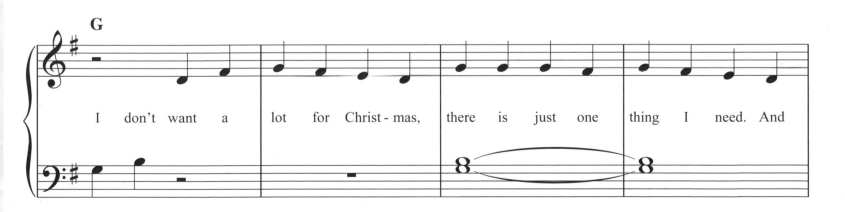

I don't want a lot for Christ-mas, there is just one thing I need. And

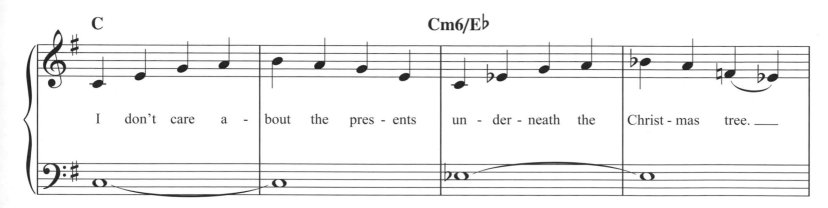

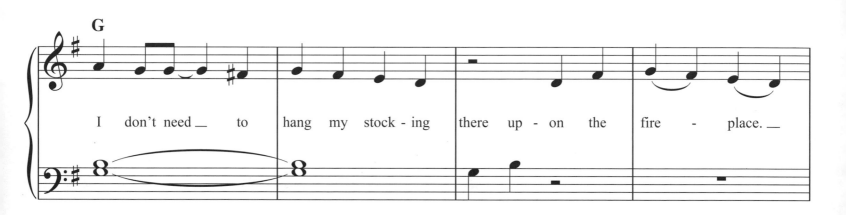

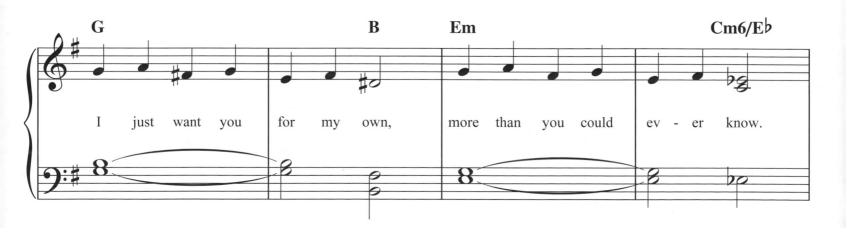

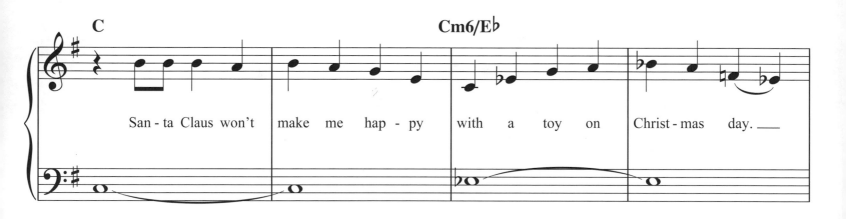

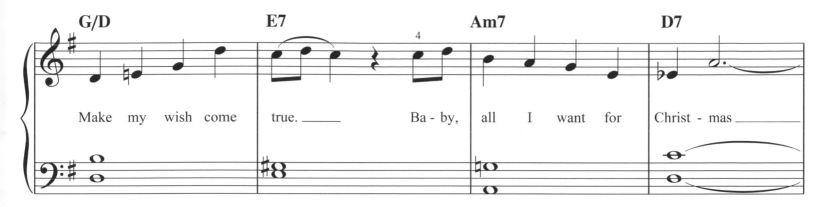

Make my wish come true.____ Ba - by, all I want for Christ - mas____

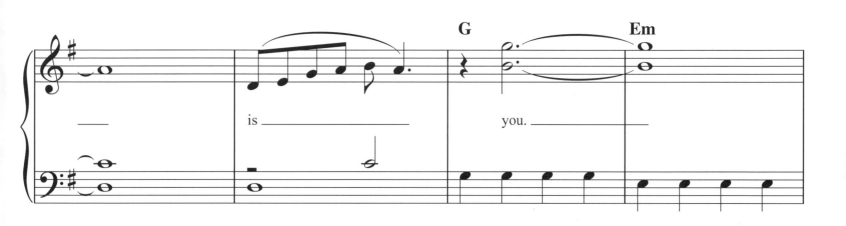

____ is_____ you._____

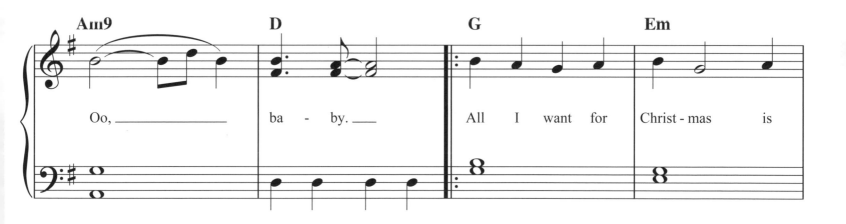

Oo,_____ ba - by.____ All I want for Christ - mas is

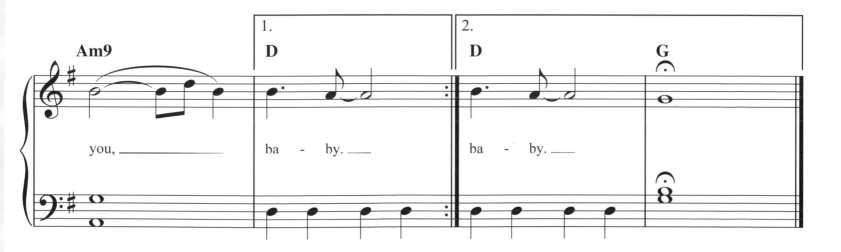

you,_____ 1. ba - by.____ 2. ba - by.____

# AULD LANG SYNE

Words by ROBERT BURNS
Traditional Scottish Melody

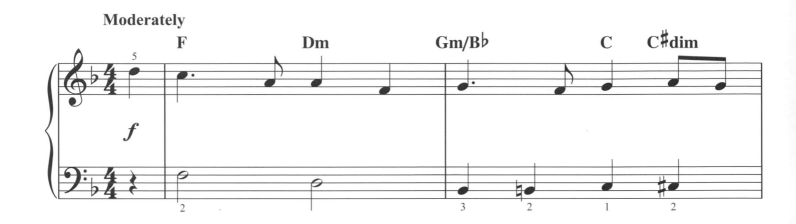

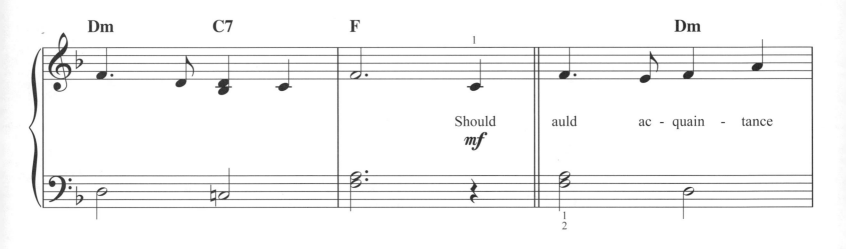

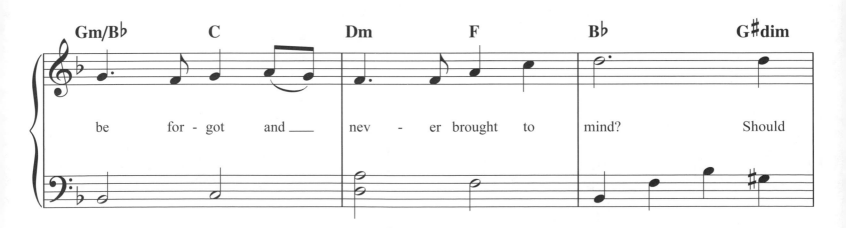

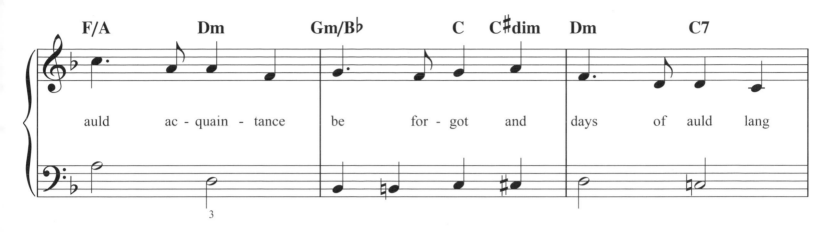

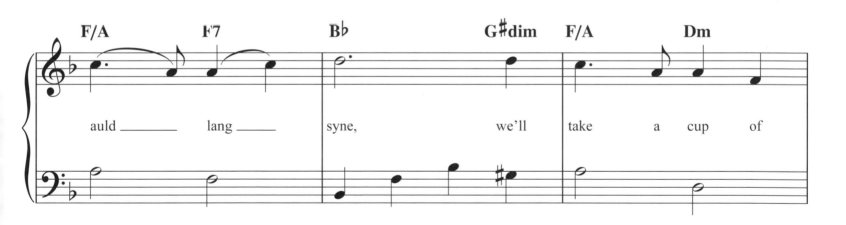

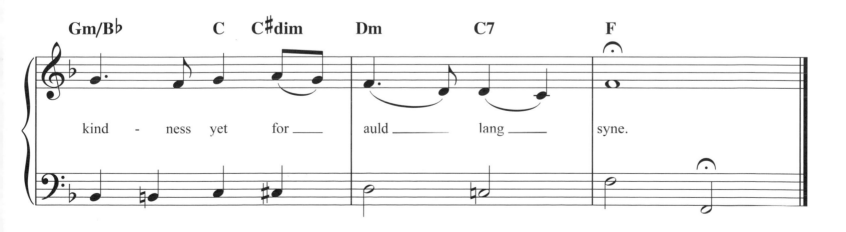

# BABY, IT'S COLD OUTSIDE

By FRANK LOESSER

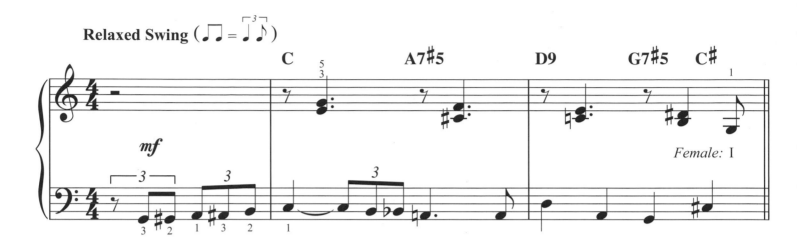

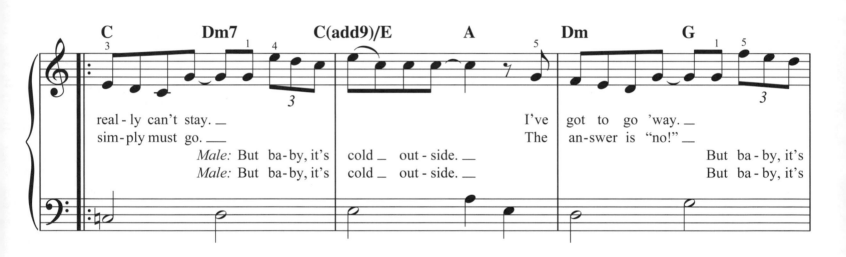

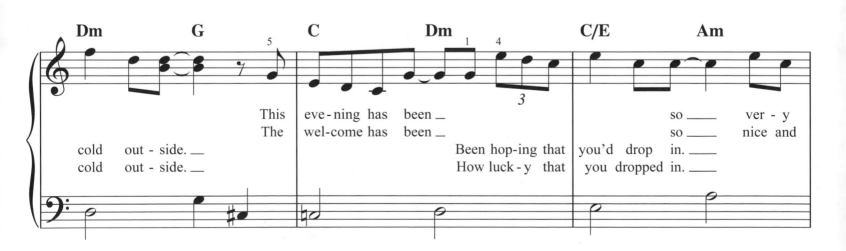

nice.
warm.
    I'll    hold    your    hands.             They're  just    like    ice.
    Look    out    the    win    -    dow ___ at    the    storm.

My    moth - er  will  start  to
My    sis - ter  will  be  sus -

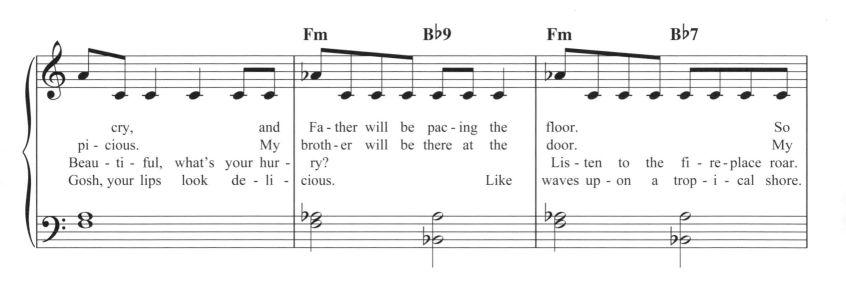

cry,              and
pi - cious.           My
Beau - ti - ful, what's your hur -
Gosh, your  lips  look  de - li -

Fa - ther will be pac - ing the
broth - er will be there at the
ry?
cious.           Like

floor.           So
door.           My
Lis - ten to the fi - re - place roar.
waves up - on  a  trop - i - cal shore.

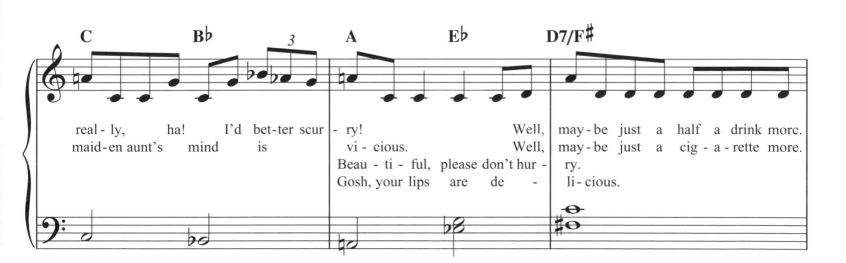

real - ly,    ha!    I'd bet - ter scur -
maid - en aunt's  mind  is

ry!               Well,
vi - cious.         Well,
Beau - ti - ful, please don't hur -
Gosh, your lips  are  de -

may - be just a half a drink more.
may - be just a cig - a - rette more.
ry.
li - cious.

ought to say, "No, no, no, sir!" At least I'm gon-na say ___ that I tried.
bound to be talk to- mor-row. At least there will be plen - ty im-plied.
Mind if I move in clos - er?
Think of my life - long sor - row

What's the sense of hurt-ing my pride? I real - ly can't stay. Oh ba - by, don't hold out.  *Both:* Ah, but it's
if you caught pneu-mo - nia and died. I real - ly can't stay. Get o - ver that old doubt.

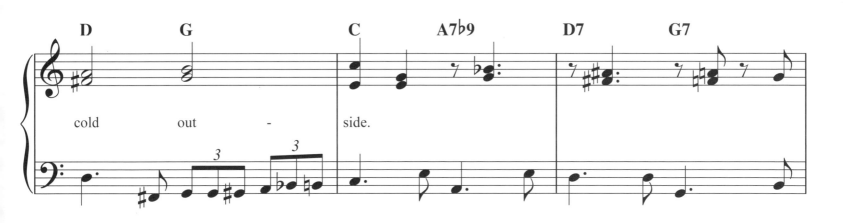

cold out - side.

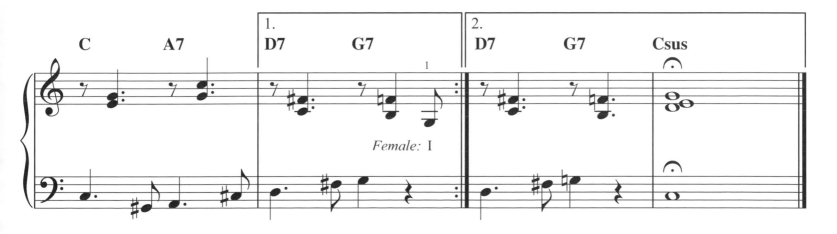

*Female:* I

# BLUE CHRISTMAS

Words and Music by BILLY HAYES
and JAY JOHNSON

**Moderately, in 2**

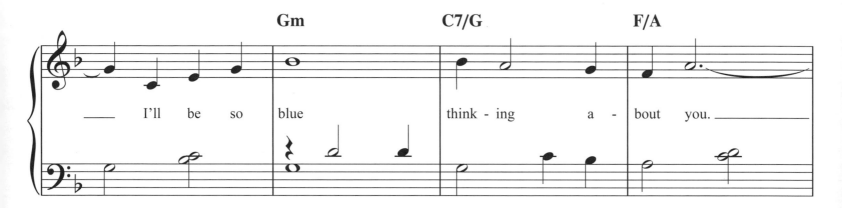

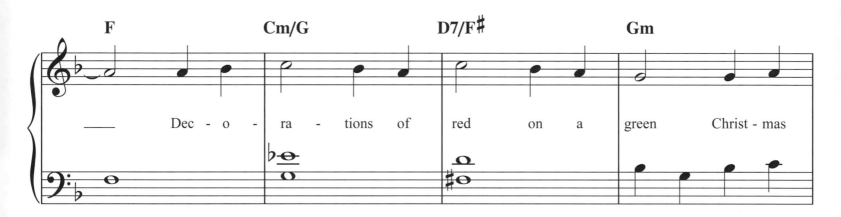

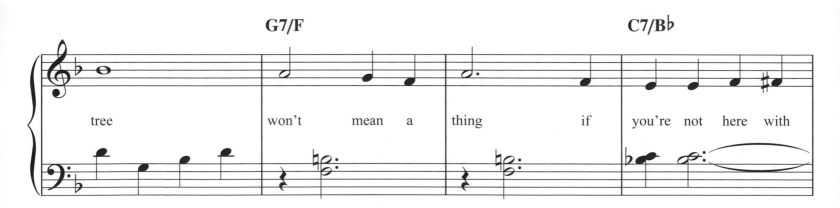

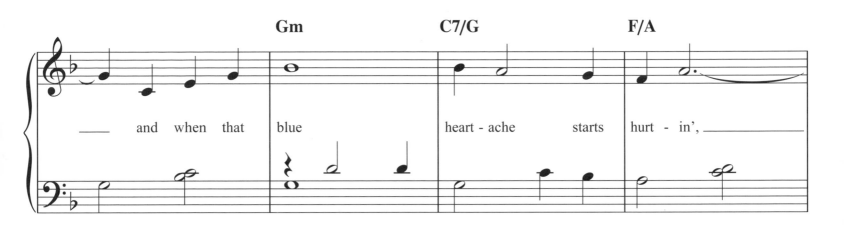

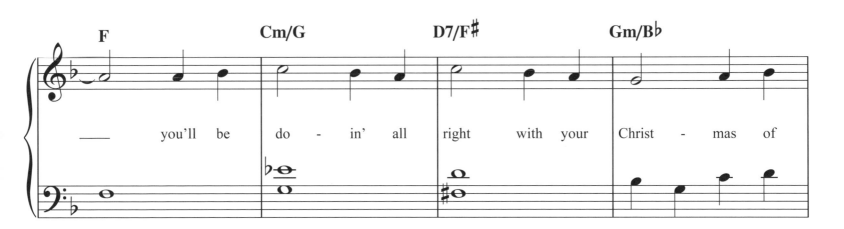

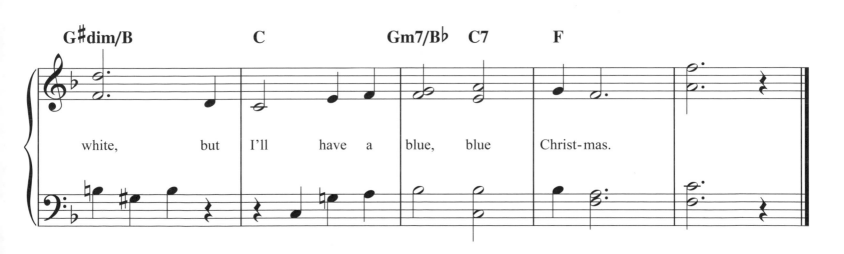

# THE CHIPMUNK SONG

Words and Music by
ROSS BAGDASARIAN

**Happily**

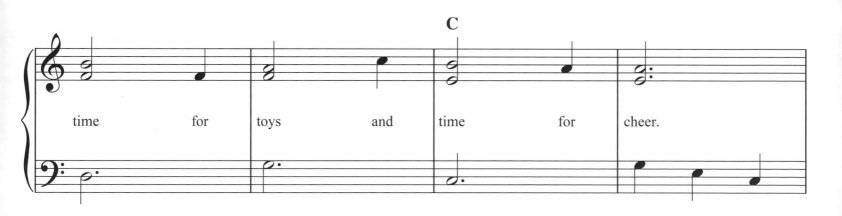

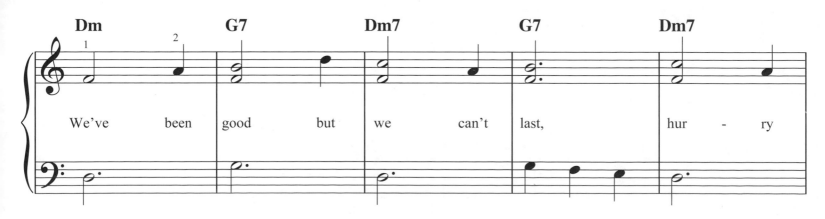

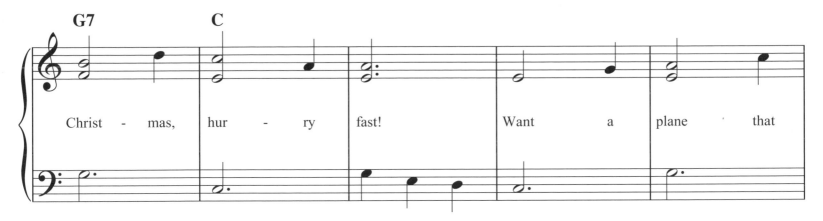

Christ - mas, hur - ry fast! Want a plane that

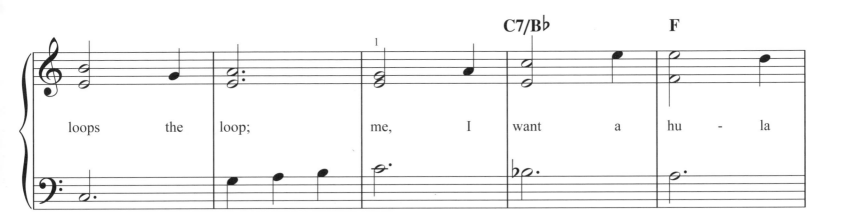

loops the loop; me, I want a hu - la

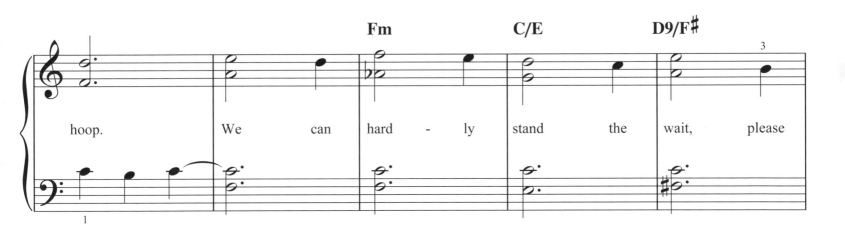

hoop. We can hard - ly stand the wait, please

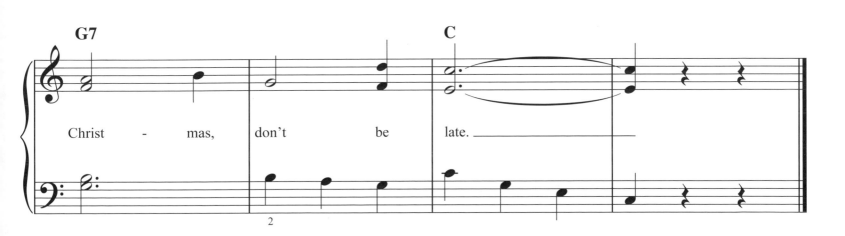

Christ - mas, don't be late. _____

# CHRISTMAS IS

Lyrics by SPENCE MAXWELL
Music by PERCY FAITH

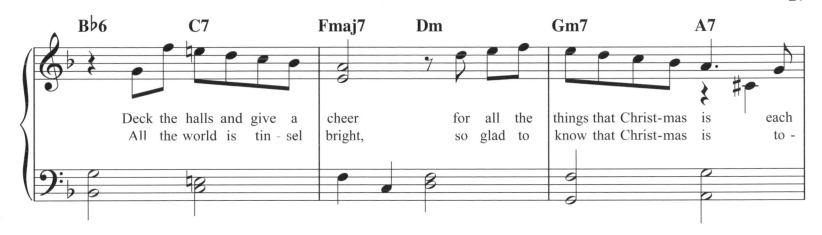

Deck the halls and give a cheer, for all the things that Christ-mas is each
All the world is tin-sel bright, so glad to know that Christ-mas is to-

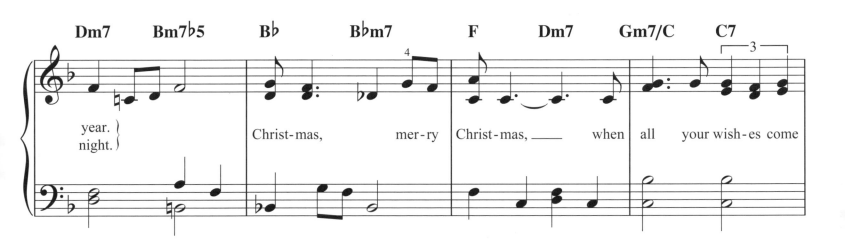

year.
night.

Christ-mas, mer-ry Christ-mas, _____ when all your wish-es come

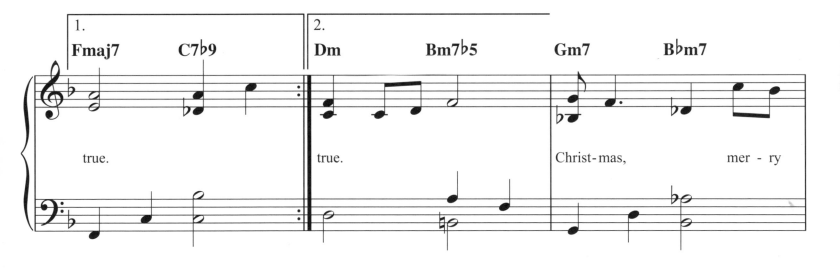

1. true.

2. true. Christ-mas, mer-ry

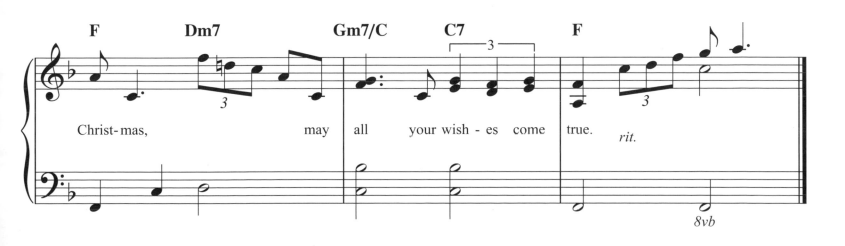

Christ-mas, may all your wish-es come true. *rit.*

*8vb*

# THE CHRISTMAS SONG
## (Chestnuts Roasting on an Open Fire)

Music and Lyric by MEL TORMÉ
and ROBERT WELLS

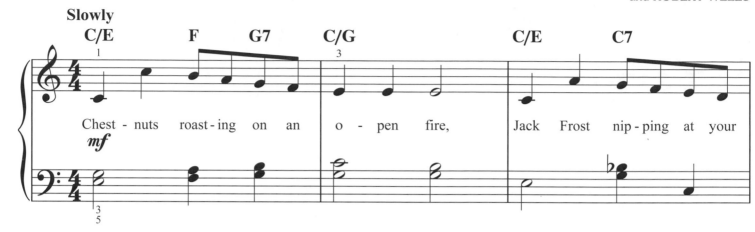

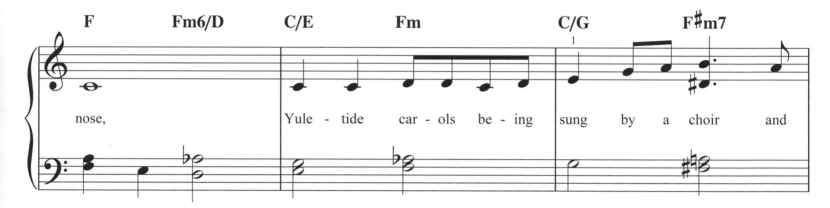

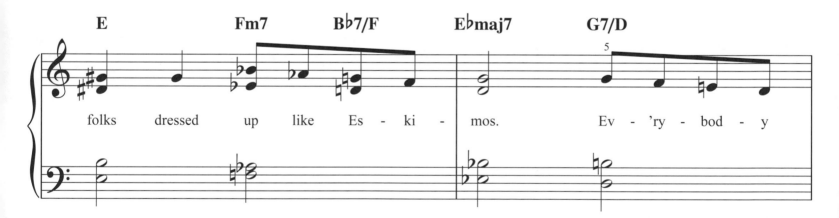

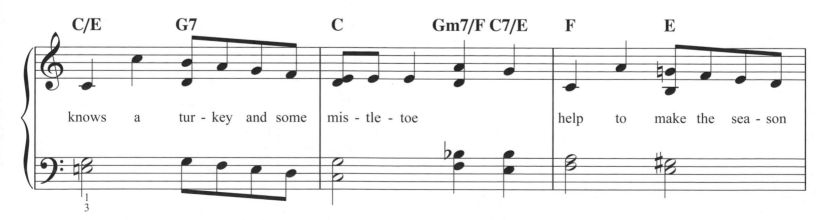

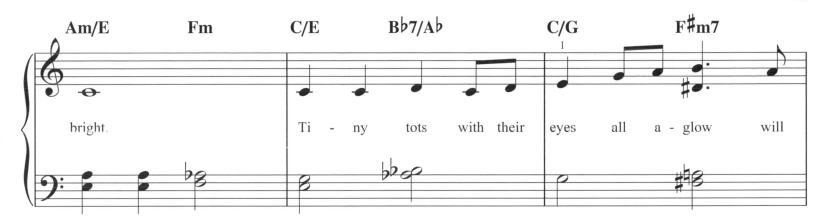

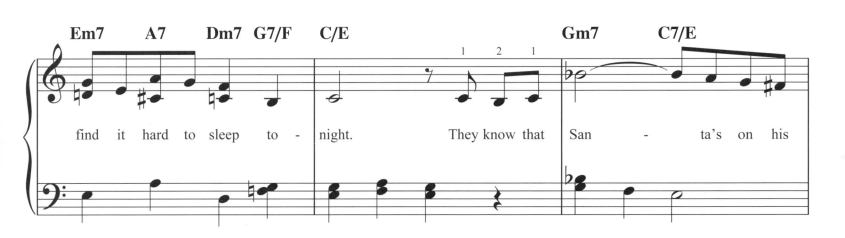

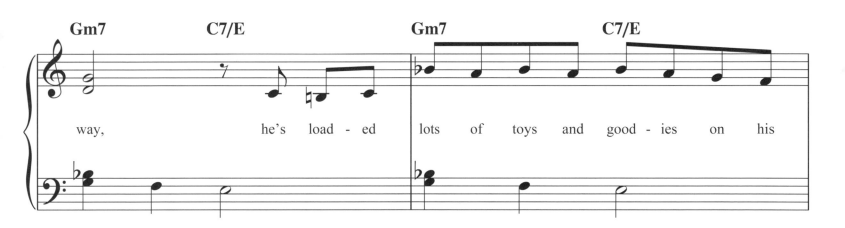

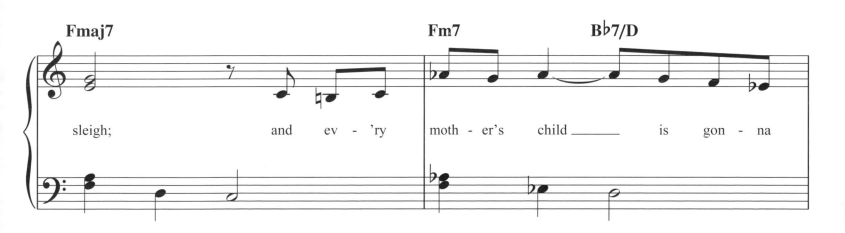

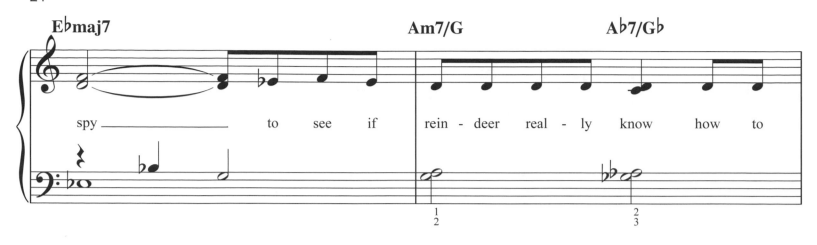

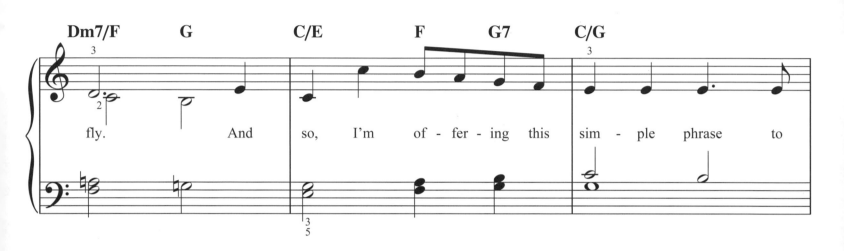

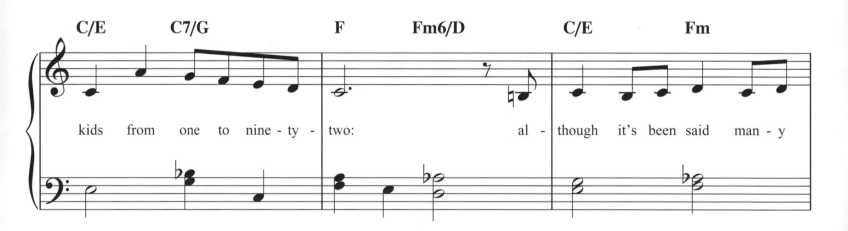

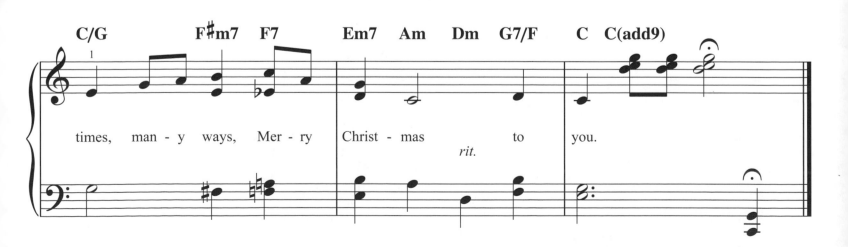

# CHRISTMAS TIME IS HERE

## from A CHARLIE BROWN CHRISTMAS

Words by LEE MENDELSON
Music by VINCE GUARALDI

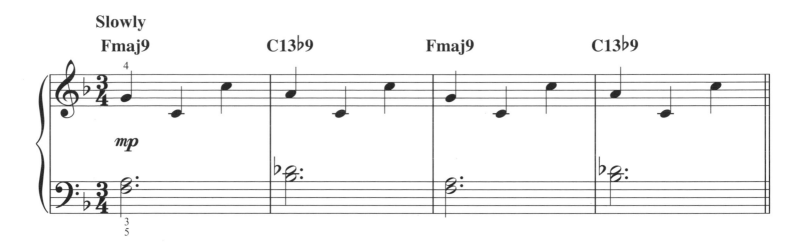

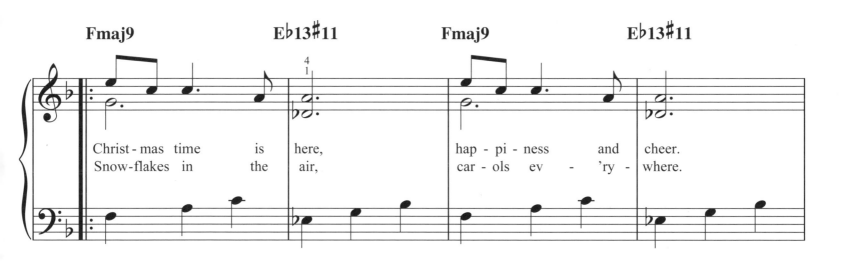

Christ-mas time    is    here,    hap - pi - ness    and    cheer.
Snow-flakes    in    the    air,    car - ols    ev    - 'ry - where.

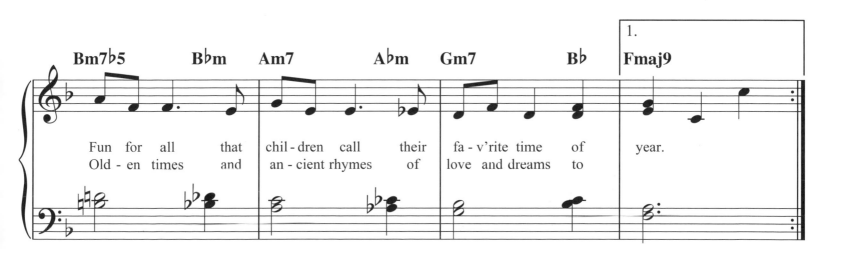

Fun    for    all    that    chil - dren    call    their    fa - v'rite    time    of    year.
Old - en    times    and    an - cient    rhymes    of    love    and    dreams    to

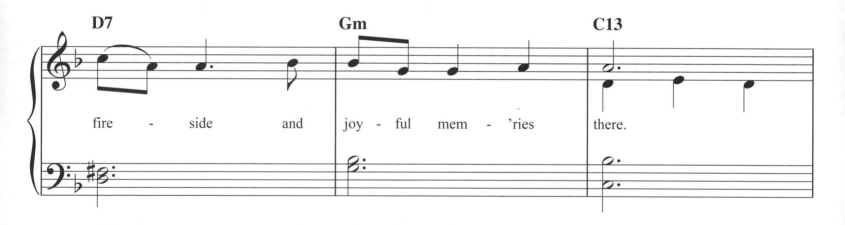

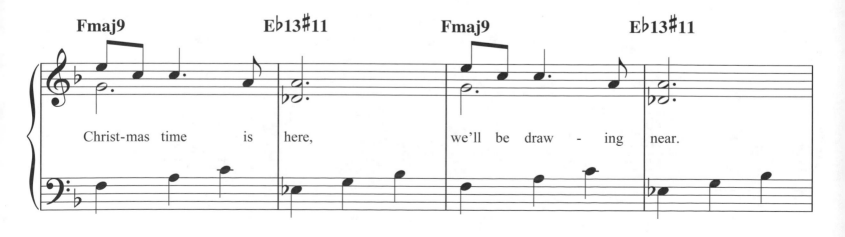

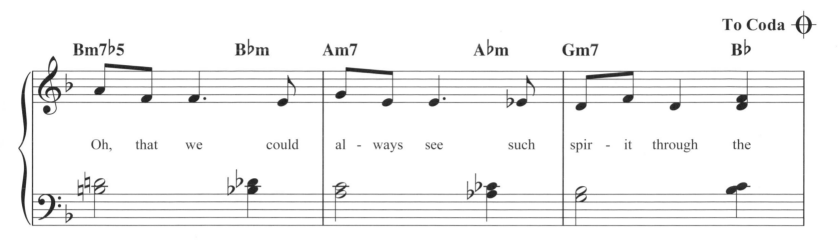

Oh, that we could al - ways see such spir - it through the

year. *Instrumental*

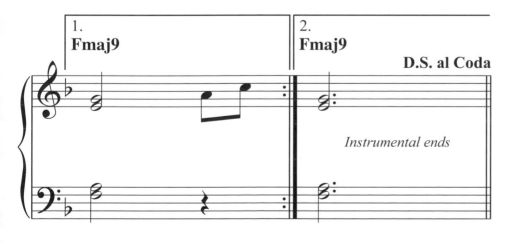

D.S. al Coda

*Instrumental ends*

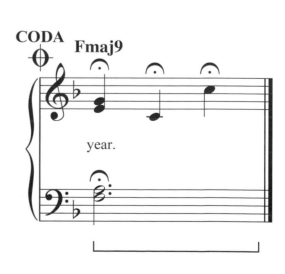

year.

# THE CHRISTMAS WALTZ

Words by SAMMY CAHN
Music by JULE STYNE

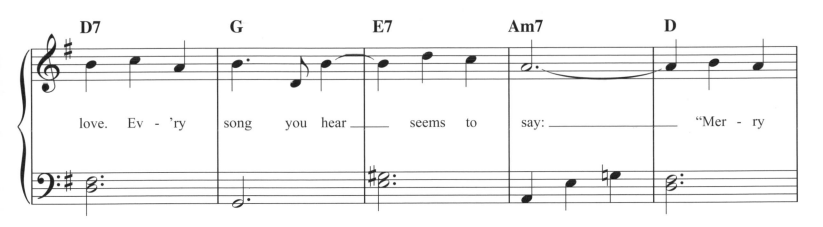

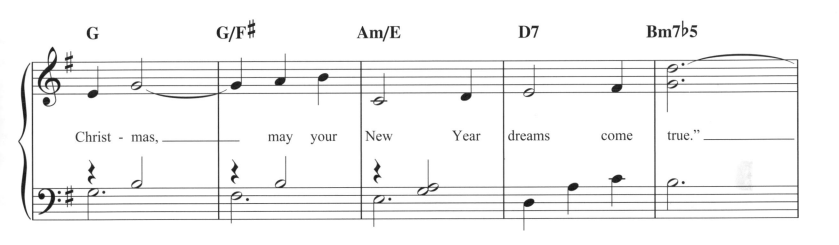

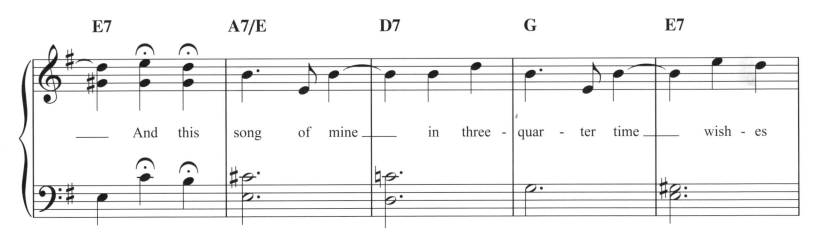

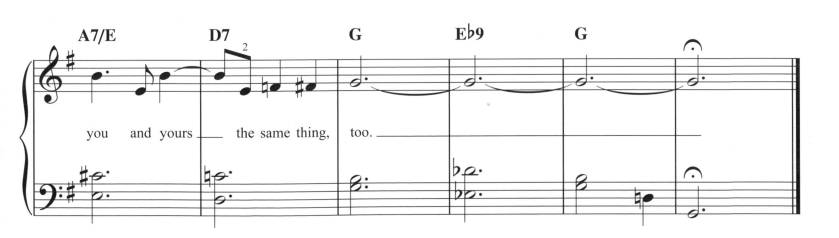

# DO YOU HEAR WHAT I HEAR

Words and Music by NOEL REGNEY
and GLORIA SHAYNE

31

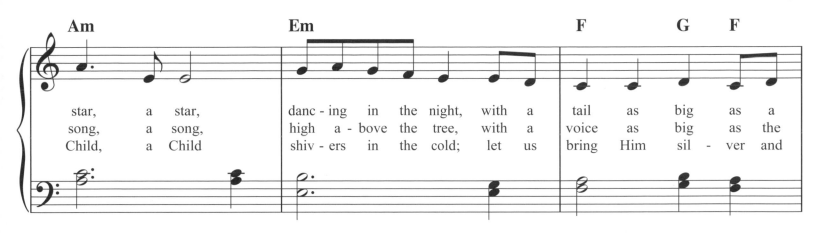

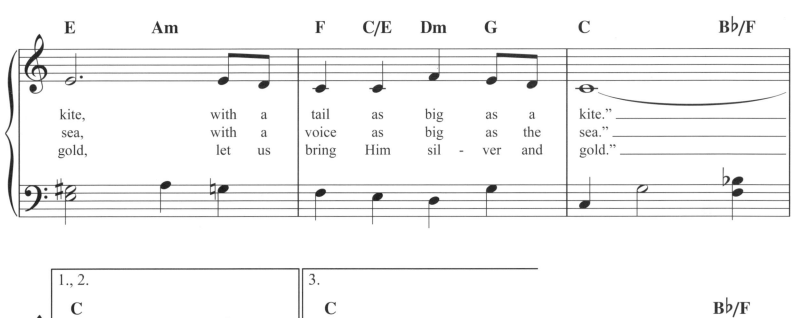

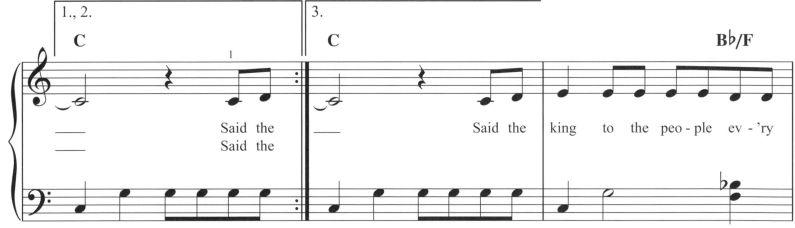

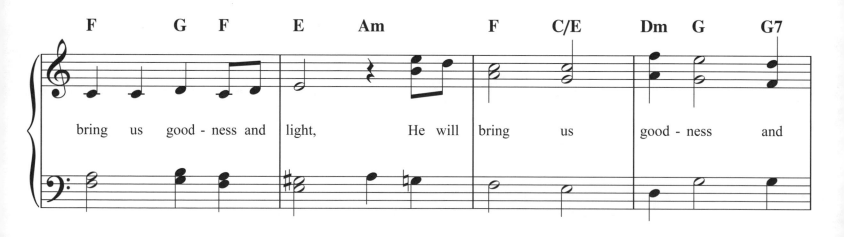

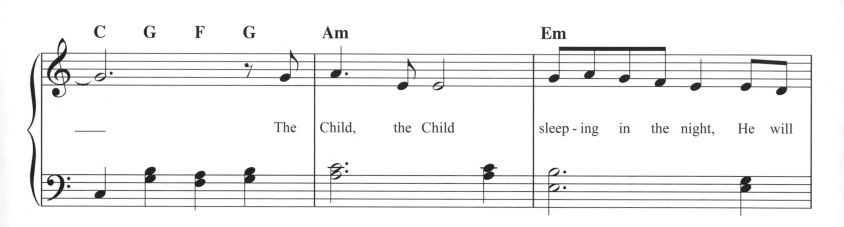

# GROWN-UP CHRISTMAS LIST

Words and Music by DAVID FOSTER
and LINDA THOMPSON-JENNER

dream. _____ So here's my life-long wish, my grown-up Christ-mas list, not
tree. _____ Well, heav-en sure-ly knows that pack-ag-es and bows can

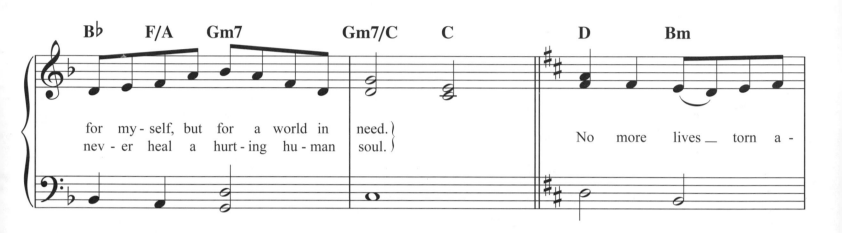

for my-self, but for a world in need.)
nev-er heal a hurt-ing hu-man soul.) No more lives — torn a-

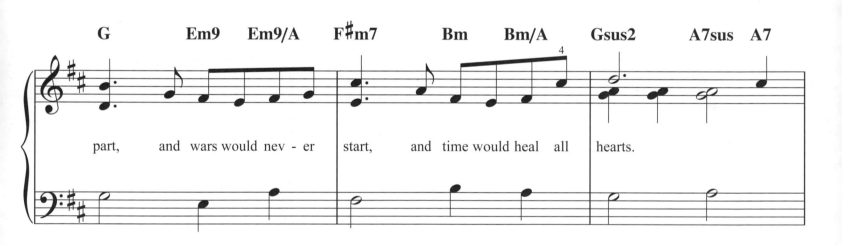

part, and wars would nev-er start, and time would heal all hearts.

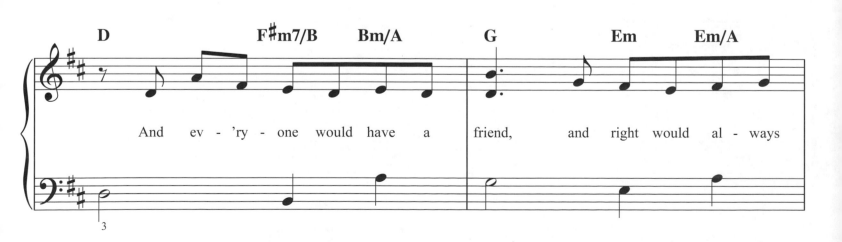

And ev-'ry-one would have a friend, and right would al-ways

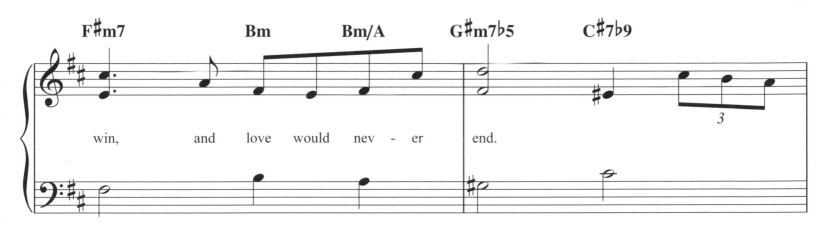

win,        and   love    would   nev - er      end.

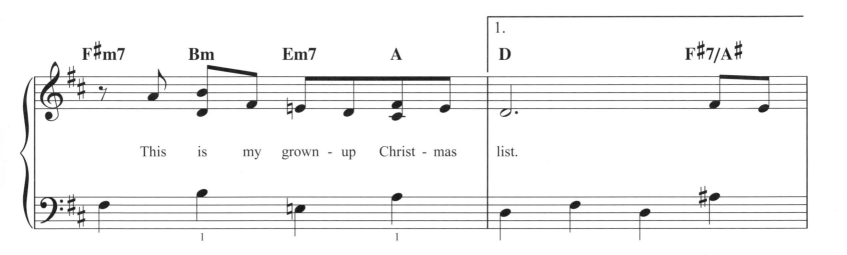

This    is    my   grown - up   Christ - mas      list.

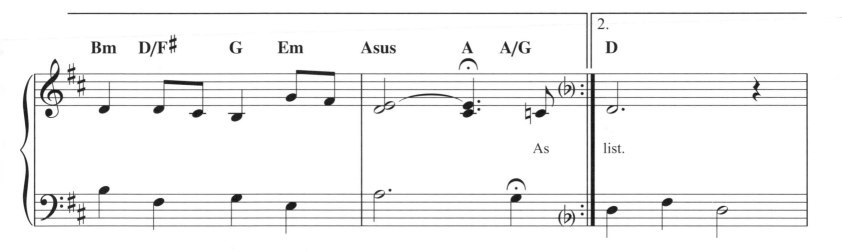

As       list.

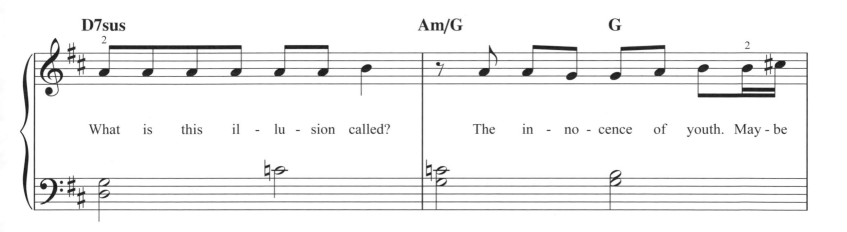

What   is   this   il - lu - sion   called?        The   in - no - cence   of   youth.   May - be

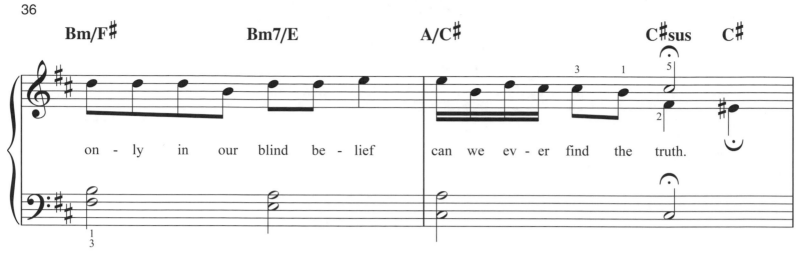

on - ly in our blind be - lief can we ev - er find the truth.

No more lives ___ torn a - part, and wars would nev - er

*mf*

start, and time would heal all hearts. And ev - 'ry - one would have a

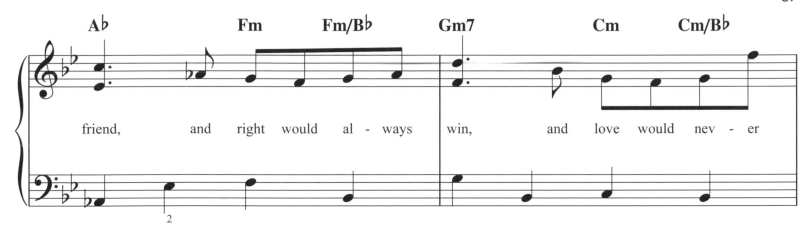

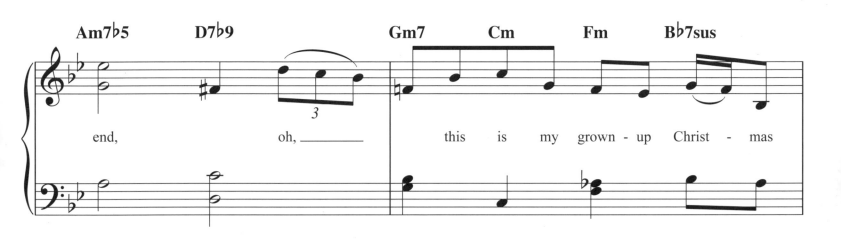

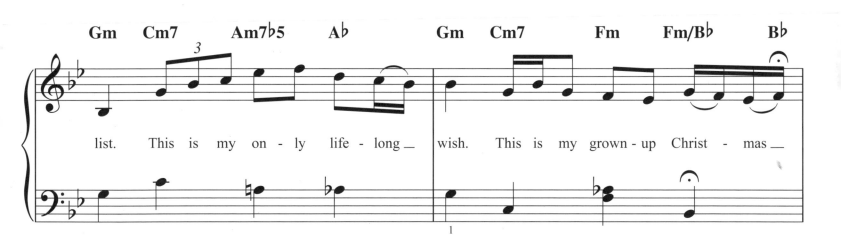

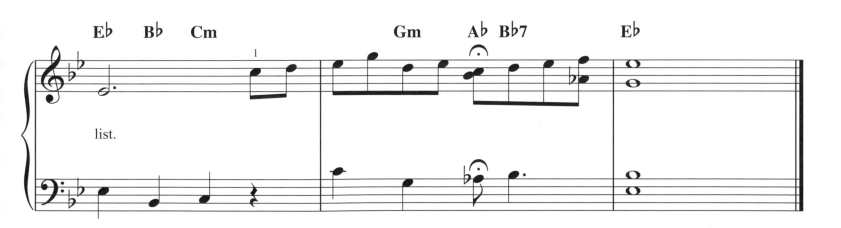

# FELIZ NAVIDAD

Music and Lyrics by
JOSÉ FELICIANO

Fe - liz Na - vi - dad. _____

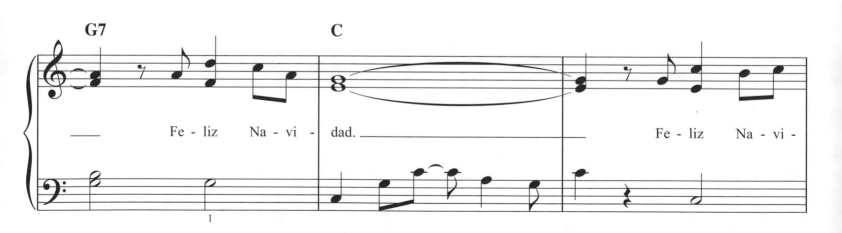

_____ Fe - liz Na - vi - dad. _____          Fe - liz Na - vi -

heart. _____     I want to wish you a Mer - ry Christ-mas

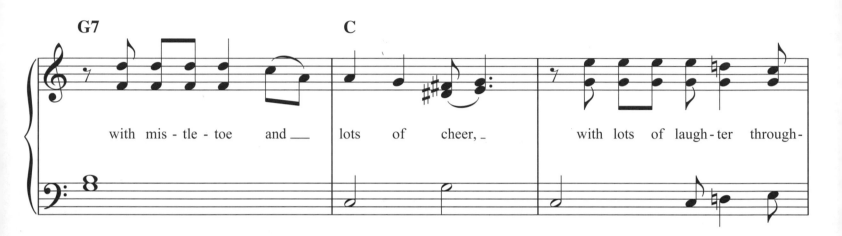

with mis - tle - toe and __ lots of cheer, _     with lots of laugh-ter through-

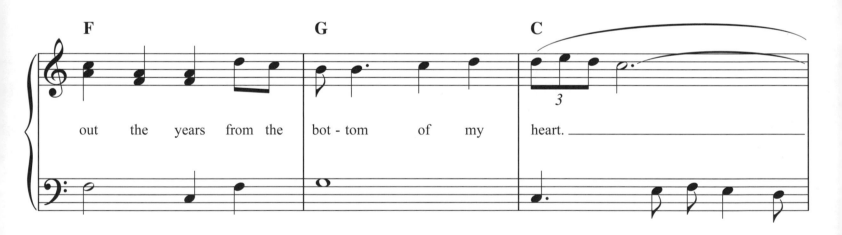

out the years from the bot - tom of my heart. _____

__ Fe - liz Na - vi -

**D.S. al Coda**

**CODA**

# HAPPY HOLIDAY
### from the Motion Picture Irving Berlin's HOLIDAY INN

Words and Music by
IRVING BERLIN

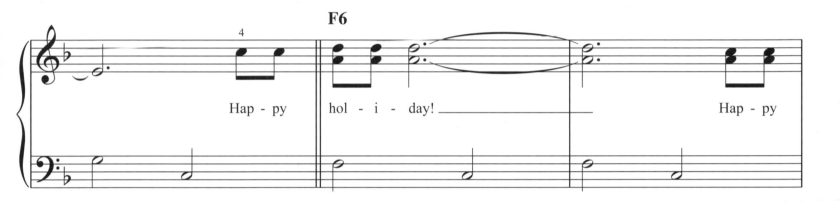

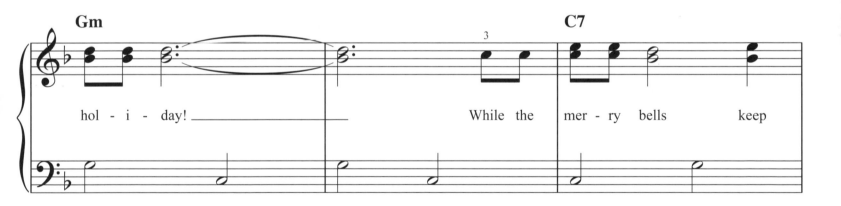

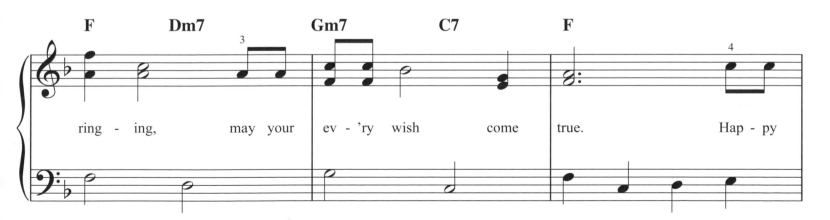

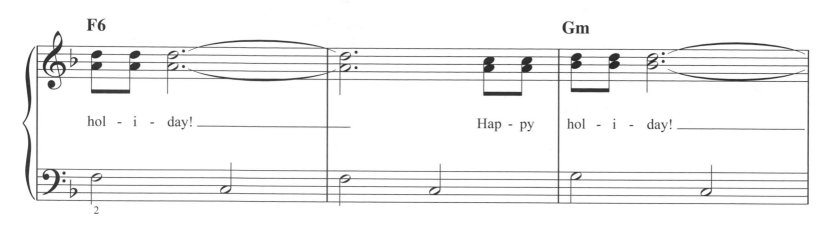

hol - i - day! _____ Hap - py hol - i - day! _____

_____ May the cal - en - dar keep bring - ing hap - py

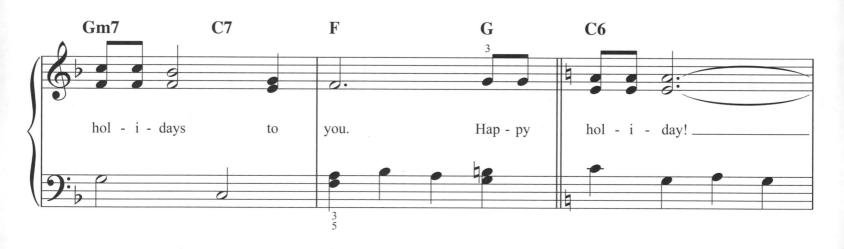

hol - i - days to you. Hap - py hol - i - day! _____

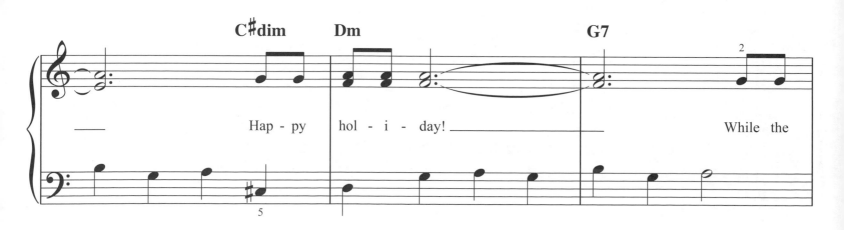

_____ Hap - py hol - i - day! _____ While the

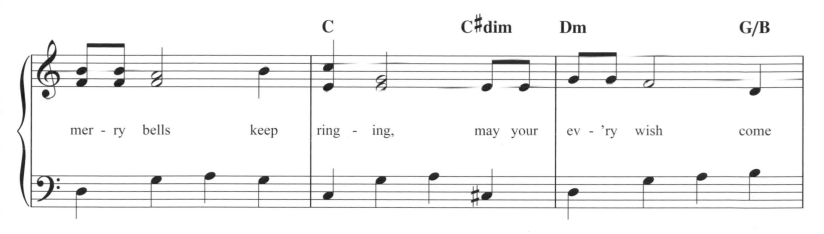

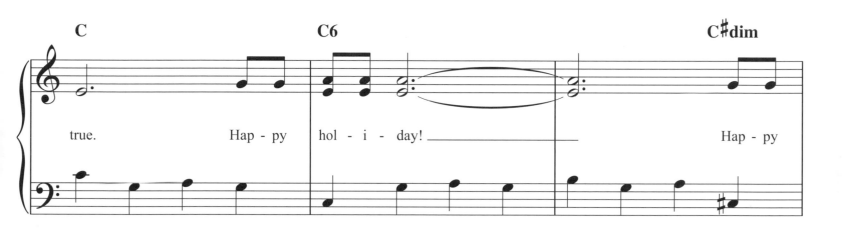

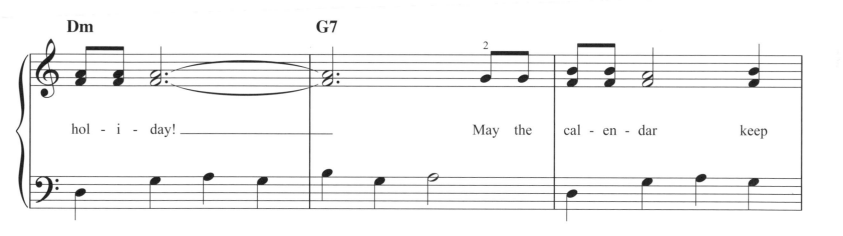

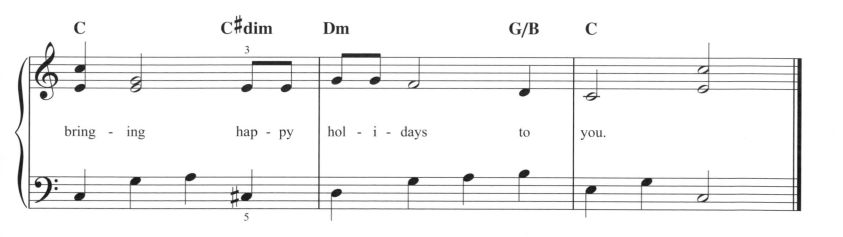

# FROSTY THE SNOW MAN

Words and Music by STEVE NELSON
and JACK ROLLINS

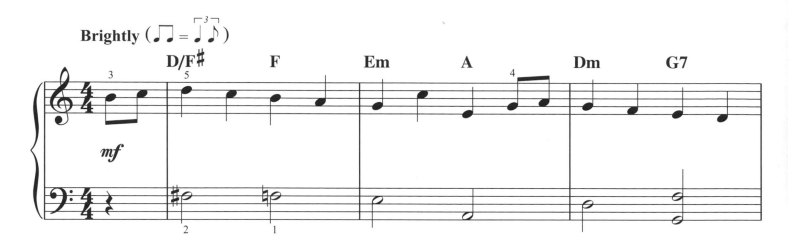

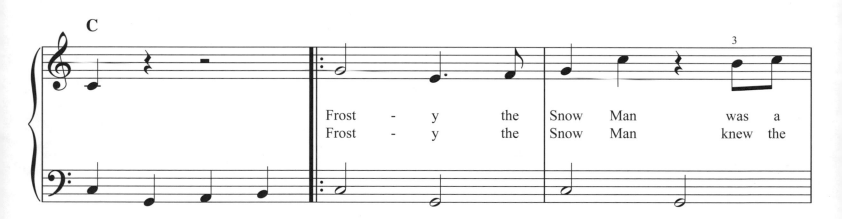

Frost - y    the    Snow Man    was a
Frost - y    the    Snow Man    knew the

jol - ly  hap - py    soul,                with a    corn - cob  pipe  and a
sun  was  hot  that    day.      So he    said, "Let's  run  and we'll

45

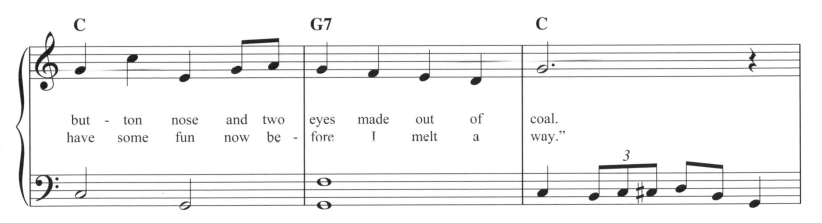

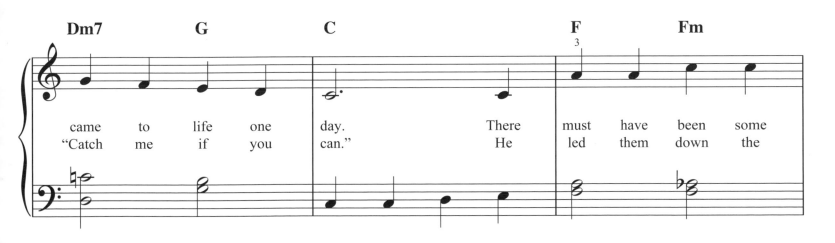

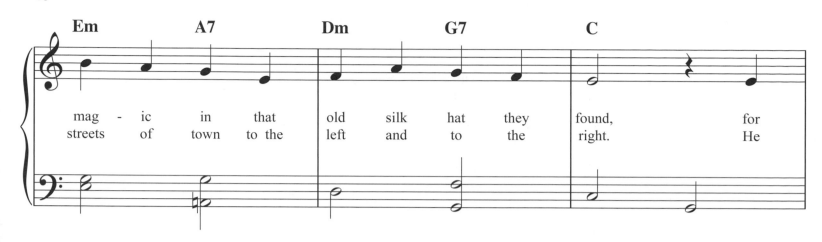

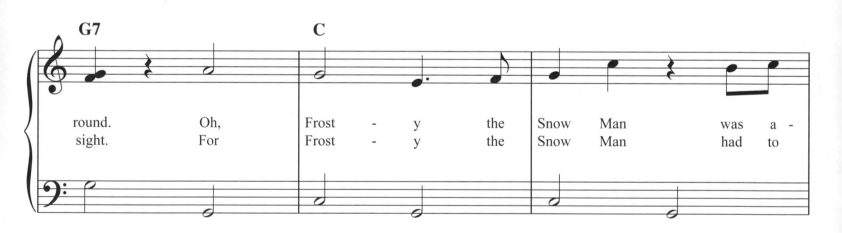

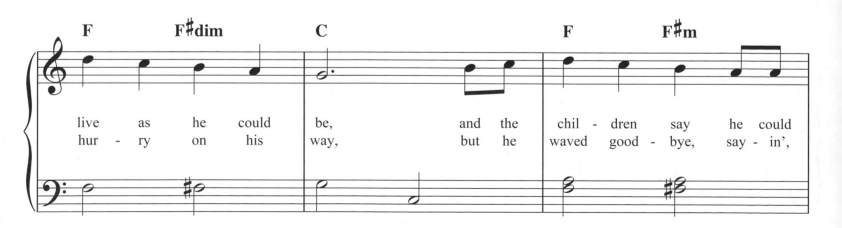

# HAPPY XMAS
## (War Is Over)

Written by JOHN LENNON
and YOKO ONO

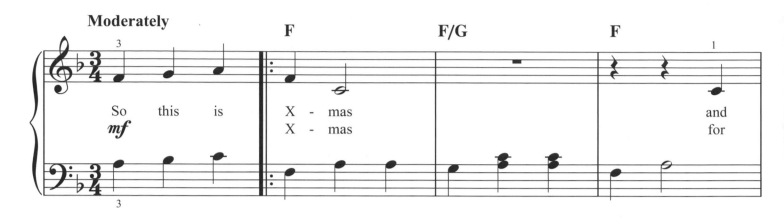

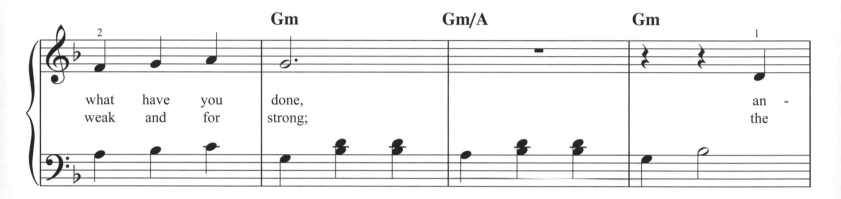

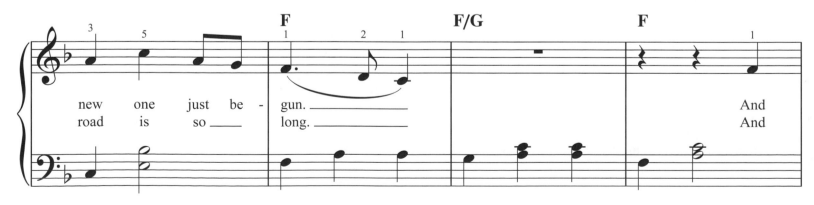

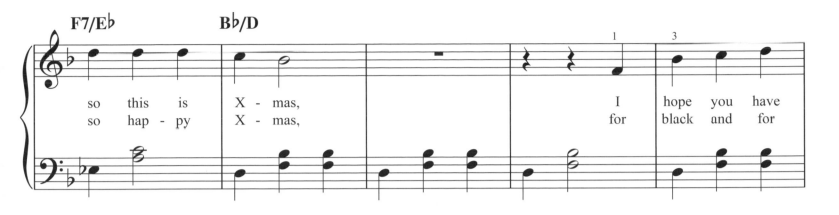

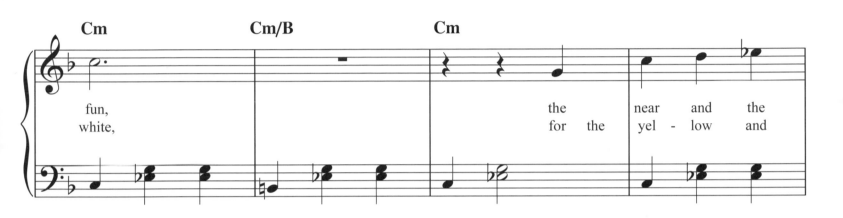

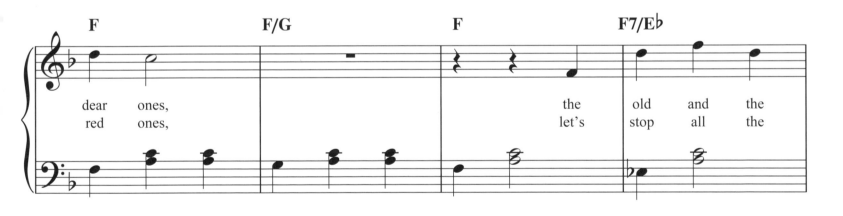

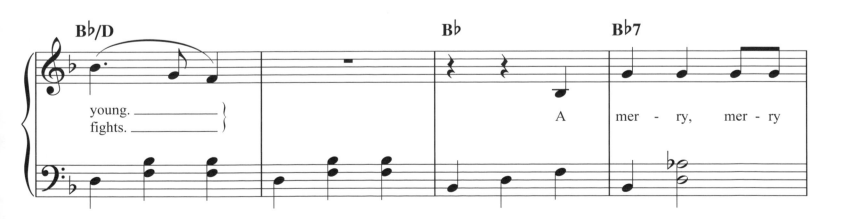

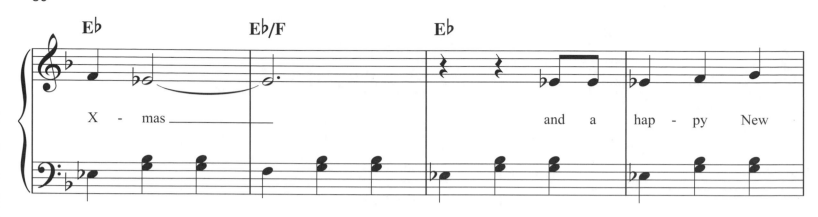

X - mas \_\_\_\_\_ and a hap - py New

Year. \_\_\_\_\_ Let's hope it's a good one, \_\_\_\_\_

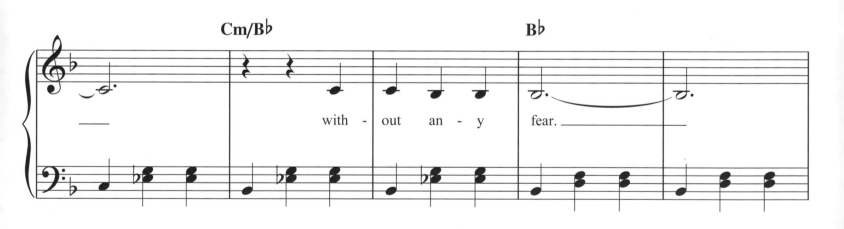

\_\_\_ with - out an - y fear. \_\_\_\_\_

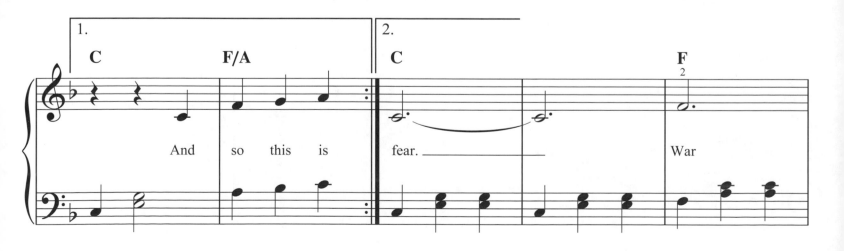

And so this is | fear. \_\_\_\_\_ War

51

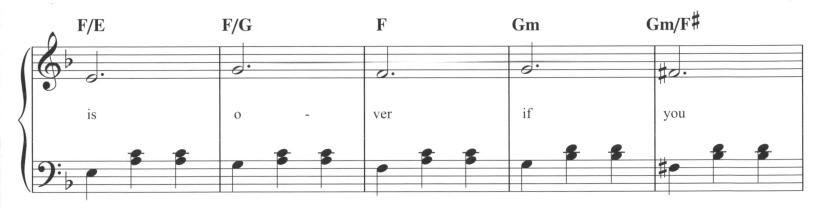

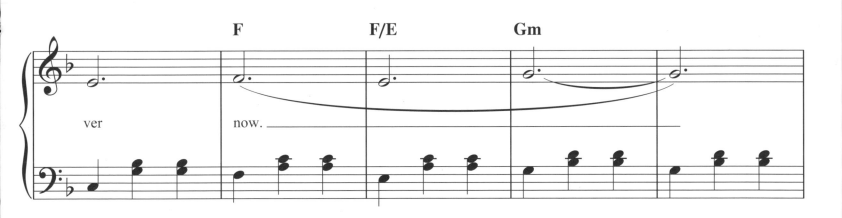

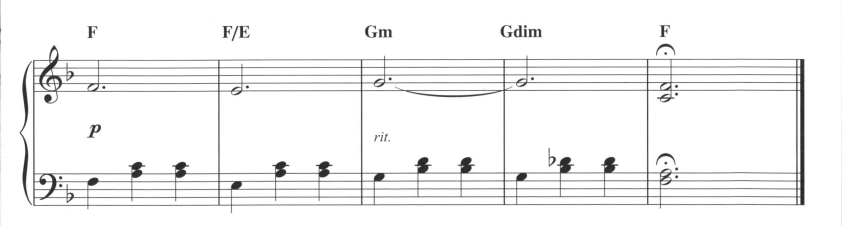

# HAVE YOURSELF A MERRY LITTLE CHRISTMAS

from MEET ME IN ST. LOUIS

Words and Music by HUGH MARTIN
and RALPH BLANE

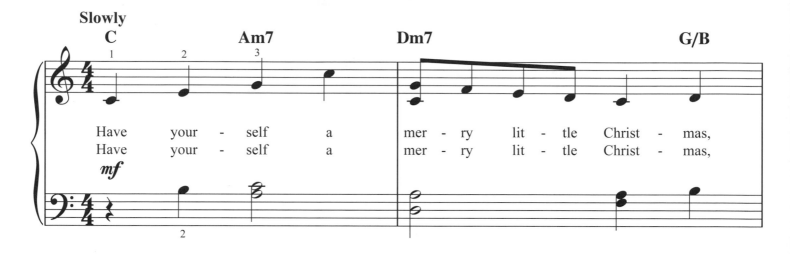

53

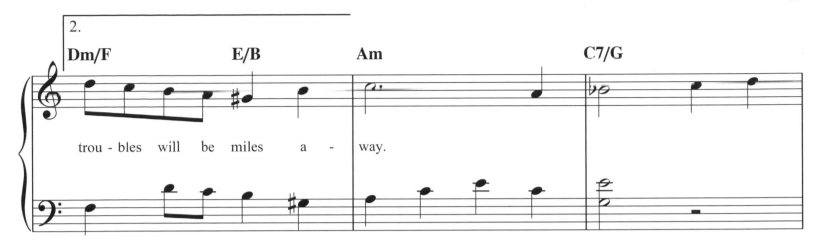

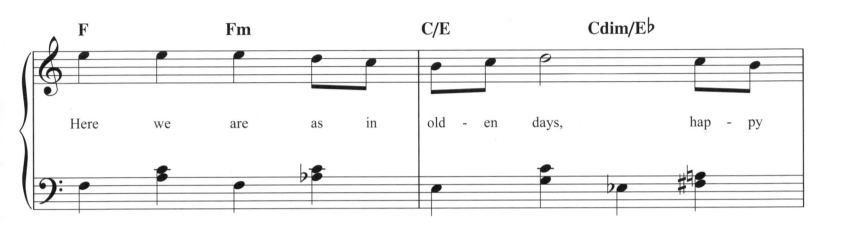

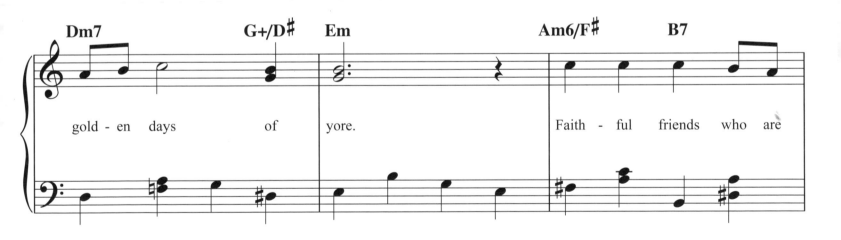

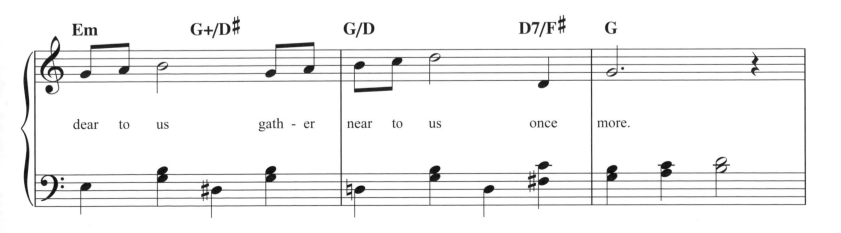

C  Am7  Dm7    G/B C/E Am7

Through the years we all will be to - geth - er, if the Fates al -

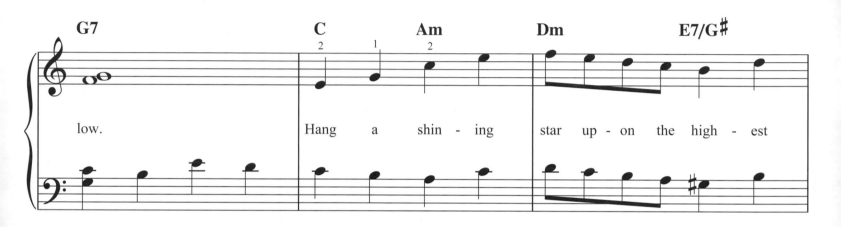

G7    C  Am  Dm  E7/G♯

low. Hang a shin - ing star up - on the high - est

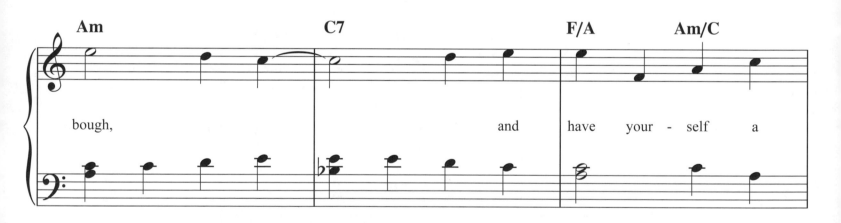

Am    C7    F/A Am/C

bough, and have your - self a

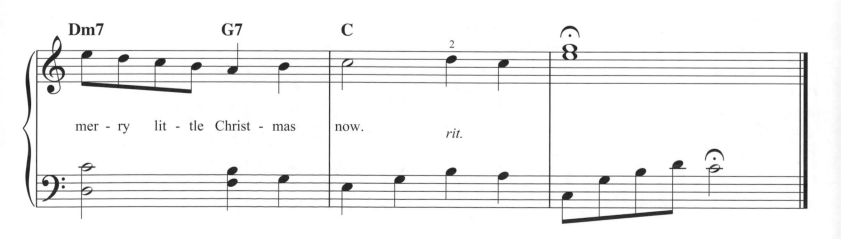

Dm7  G7  C

mer - ry lit - tle Christ - mas now. *rit.*

# A HOLLY JOLLY CHRISTMAS

Music and Lyrics by
JOHNNY MARKS

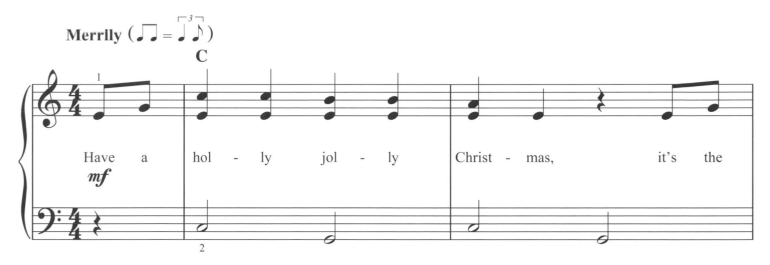

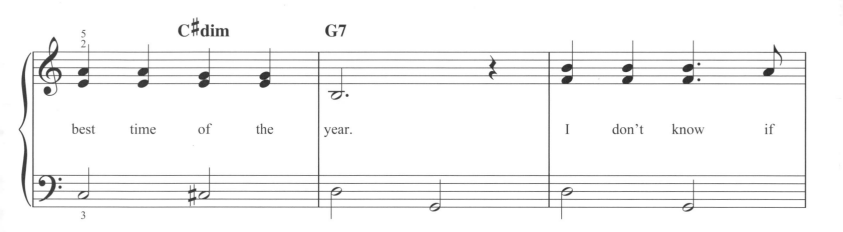

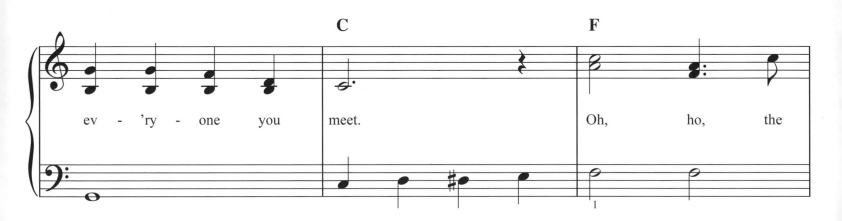

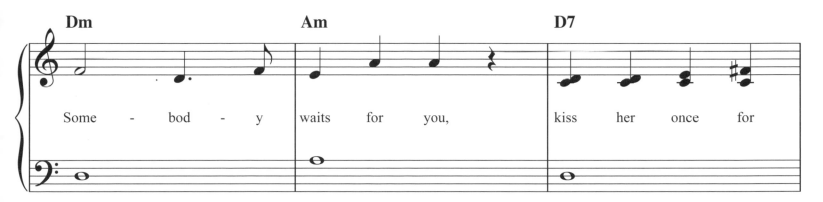

**Dm**　　　　　　　　　　　　**Am**　　　　　　　　　　　**D7**

Some - bod - y　waits　for　you,　　　kiss　her　once　for

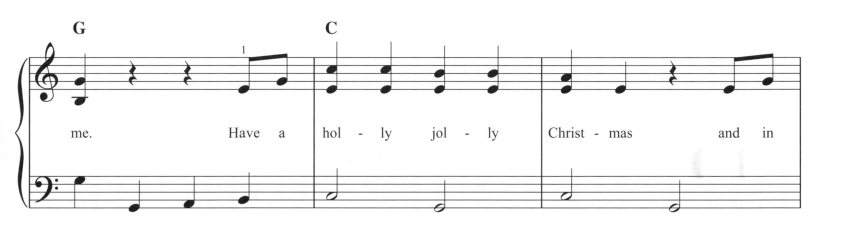

**G**　　　　　　　　　　　　　**C**

me.　　　Have　a　hol - ly　jol - ly　Christ - mas　　　and　in

**C#dim**　　**G7**

case　you　did - n't　hear,　　　oh　by　gol - ly,　have　a

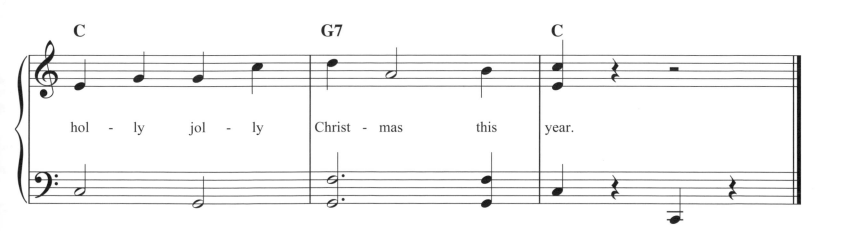

**C**　　　　　　　　　　　**G7**　　　　　　　　　**C**

hol - ly　jol - ly　Christ - mas　this　year.

# HERE COMES SANTA CLAUS

## (Right Down Santa Claus Lane)

Words and Music by GENE AUTRY
and OAKLEY HALDEMAN

Here comes San - ta Claus! Here comes San - ta Claus!

Right down San - ta Claus Lane!

Vix - en and Blitz - en and
He's got a bag that is
He does - n't care if you're
He'll come a - round when the

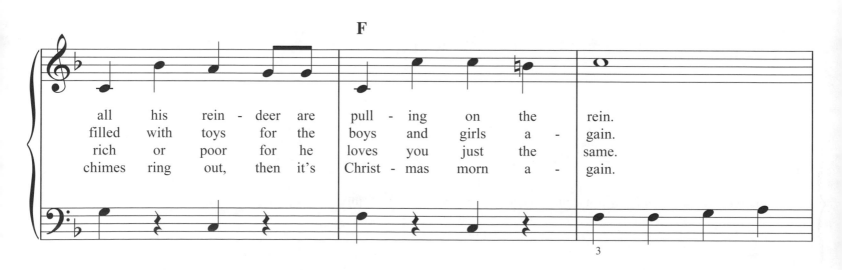

all his rein - deer are pull - ing on the rein.
filled with toys for the boys and girls a - gain.
rich or poor for he loves you just the same.
chimes ring out, then it's Christ - mas morn a - gain.

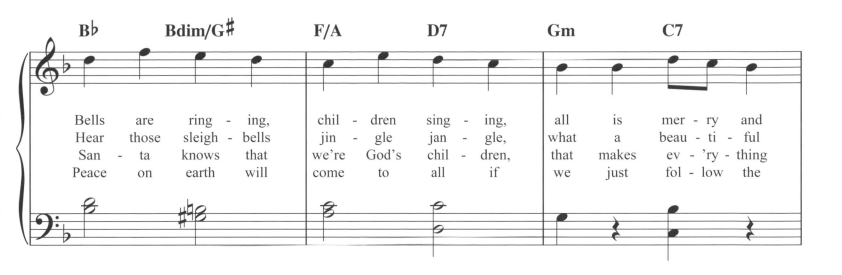

Bells are ring - ing, chil - dren sing - ing, all is mer - ry and
Hear those sleigh - bells jin - gle jan - gle, what a beau - ti - ful
San - ta knows that we're God's chil - dren, that makes ev - 'ry - thing
Peace on earth will come to all if we just fol - low the

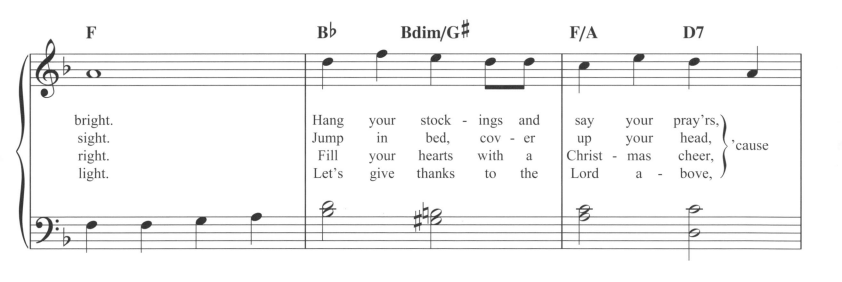

bright.
sight.
right.
light.

Hang your stock - ings and say your pray'rs,
Jump in bed, cov - er up your head,          'cause
Fill your hearts with a Christ - mas cheer,
Let's give thanks to the Lord a - bove,

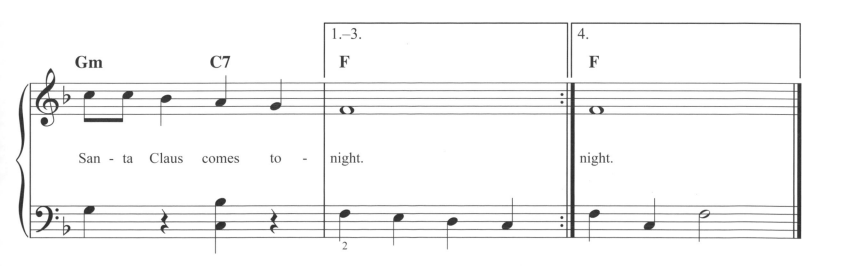

San - ta Claus comes to - night.

night.

(There's No Place Like)
# HOME FOR THE HOLIDAYS

Words and Music by AL STILLMAN
and ROBERT ALLEN

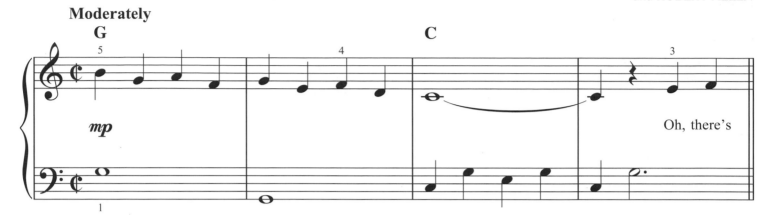

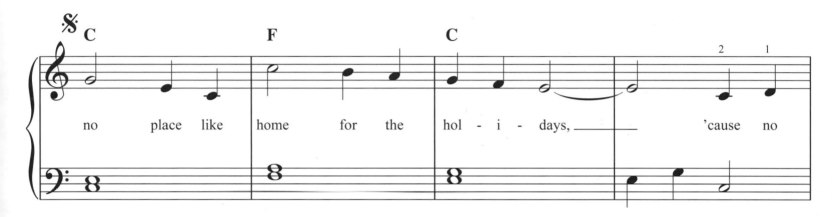

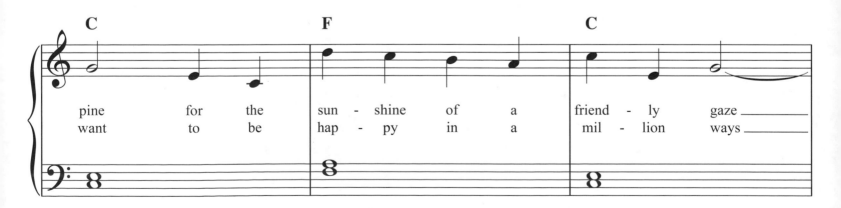

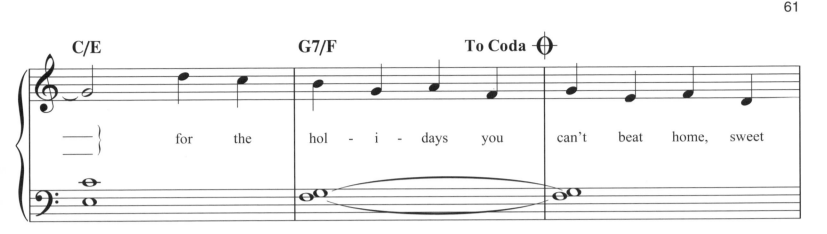

C/E                  G7/F             To Coda

for the hol - i - days you can't beat home, sweet

C                          F      E      F      E

home.           I met a man who lives in Ten - nes - see and

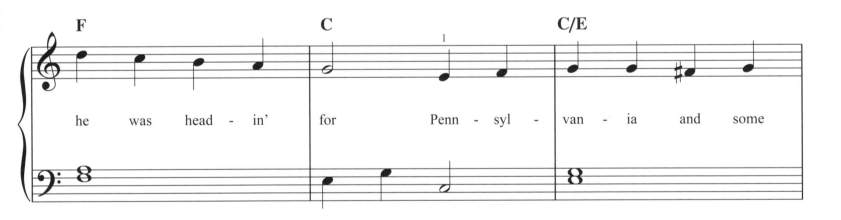

F                   C                   C/E

he was head - in' for Penn - syl - van - ia and some

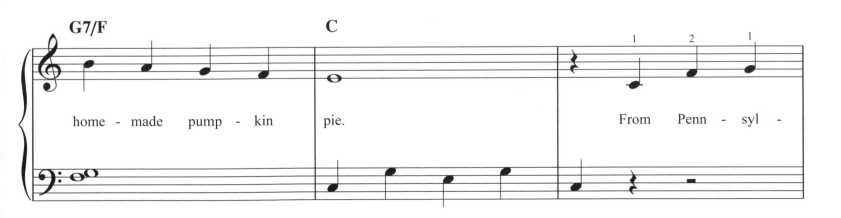

G7/F                C

home - made pump - kin pie.              From Penn - syl -

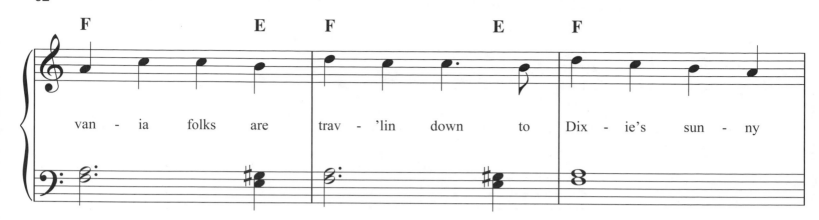

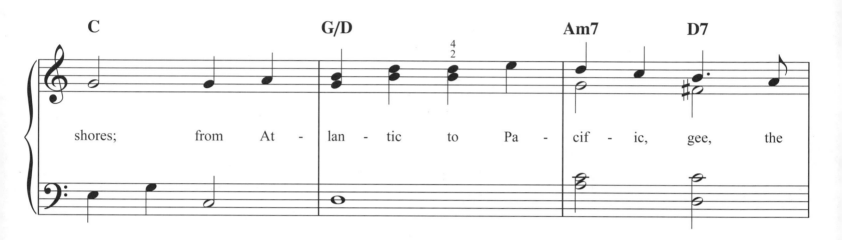

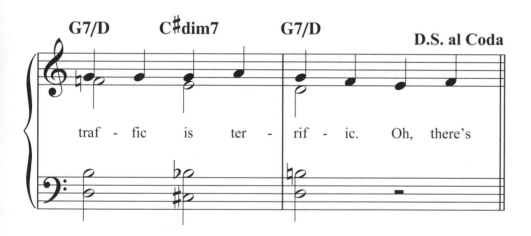

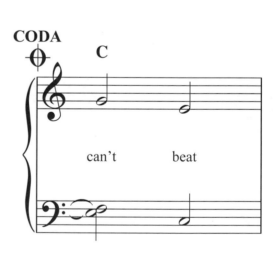

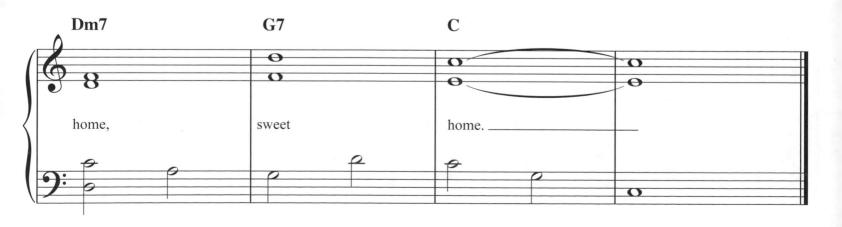

# I HEARD THE BELLS ON CHRISTMAS DAY

Words by HENRY WADSWORTH LONGFELLOW
Adapted by JOHNNY MARKS
Music by JOHNNY MARKS

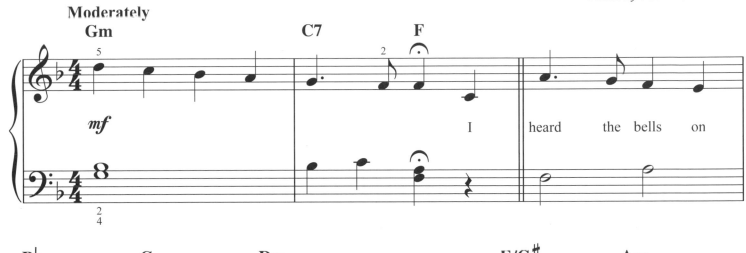

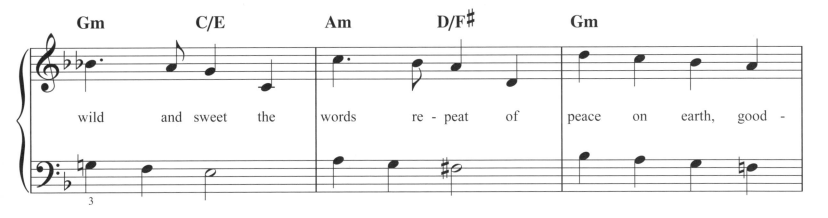

bel - fries of all Chris - ten - dom had rung so long the un -

bro - ken song of peace on earth good - will to men.

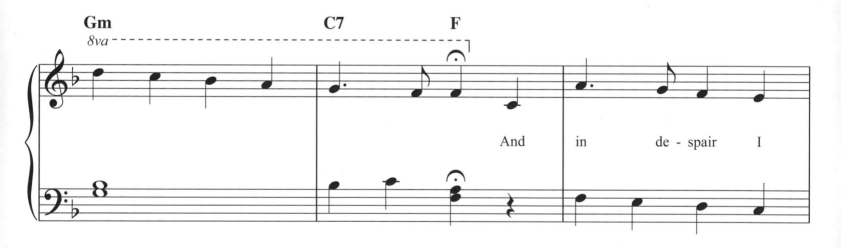

And in de - spair I

bowed my head. "There is no peace on earth," I said. "For

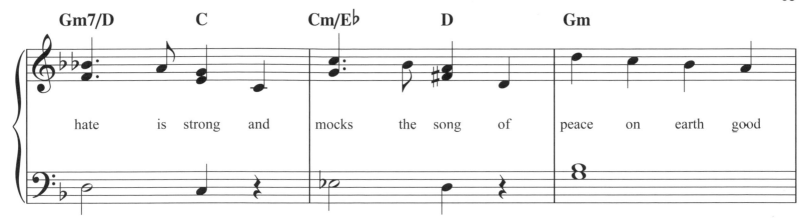

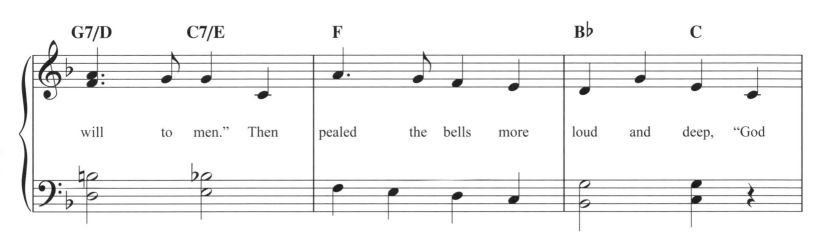

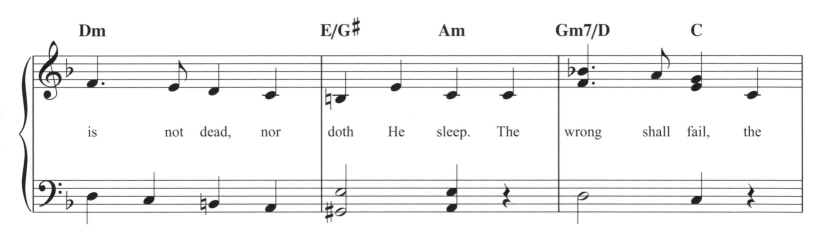

# I SAW MOMMY KISSING SANTA CLAUS

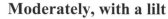

Words and Music by
TOMMIE CONNOR

**Moderately, with a lilt**

I saw Mom-my kiss-ing San - ta Claus

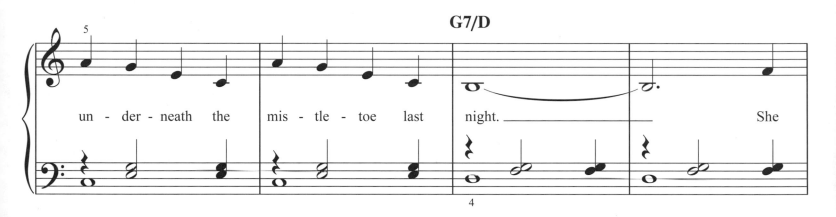

un-der-neath the mis-tle-toe last night. _____ She

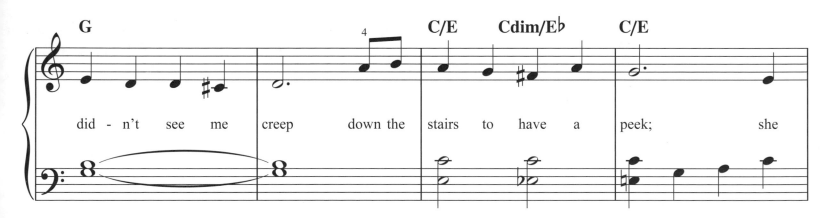

did-n't see me creep down the stairs to have a peek; she

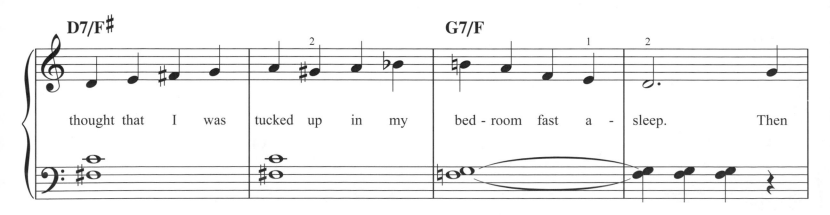

thought that I was tucked up in my bed-room fast a - sleep. Then

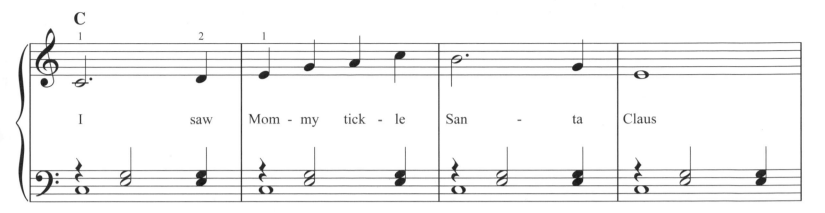

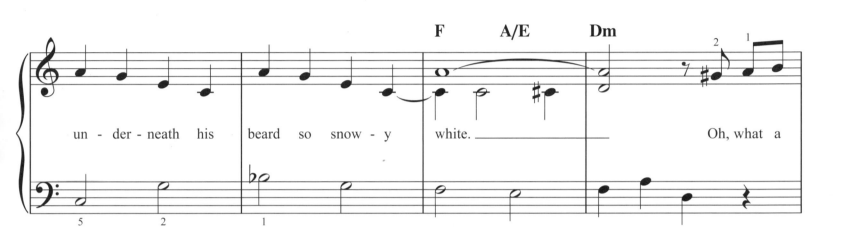

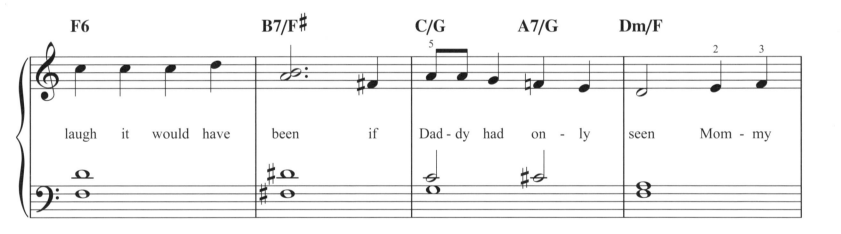

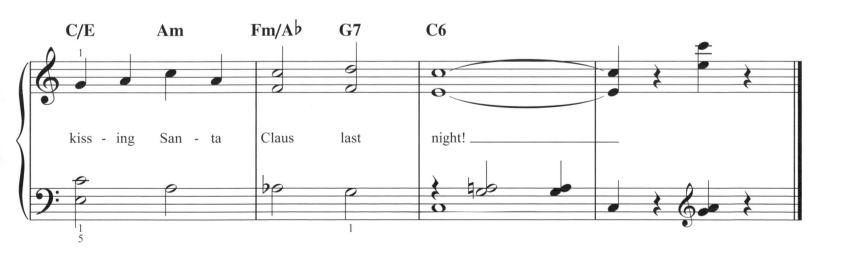

# I WONDER AS I WANDER

By JOHN JACOB NILES

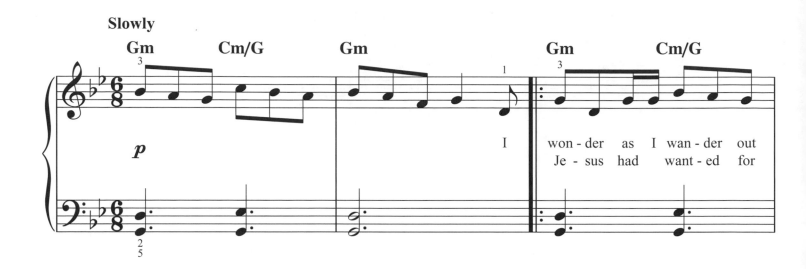

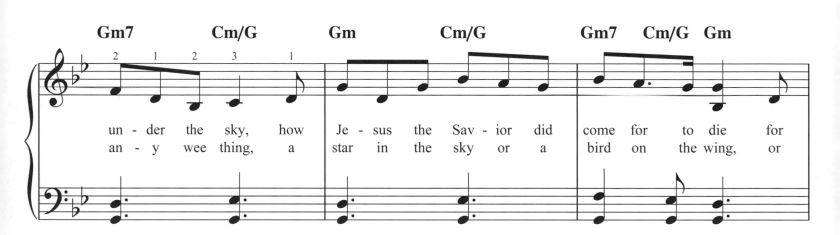

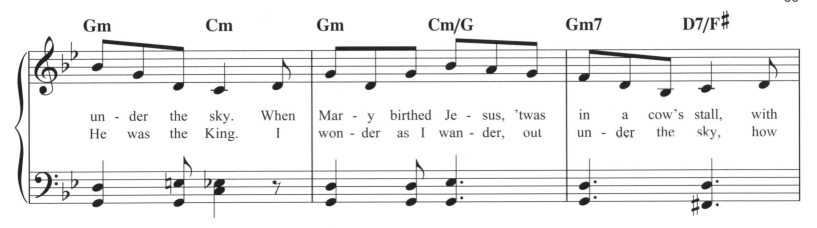

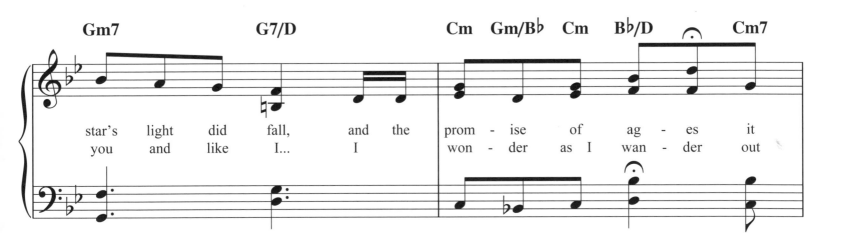

# I'LL BE HOME FOR CHRISTMAS

Words and Music by KIM GANNON
and WALTER KENT

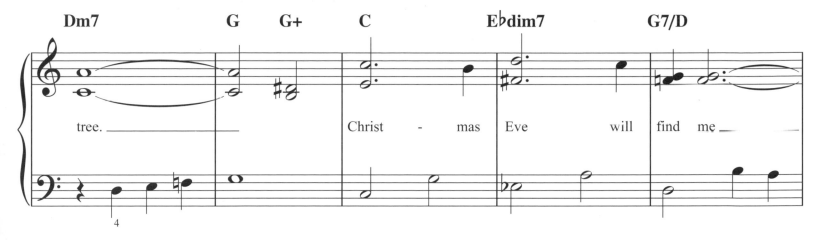

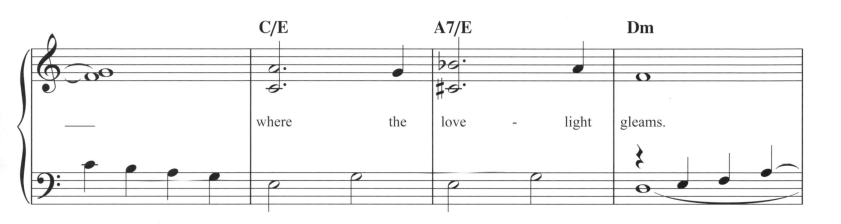

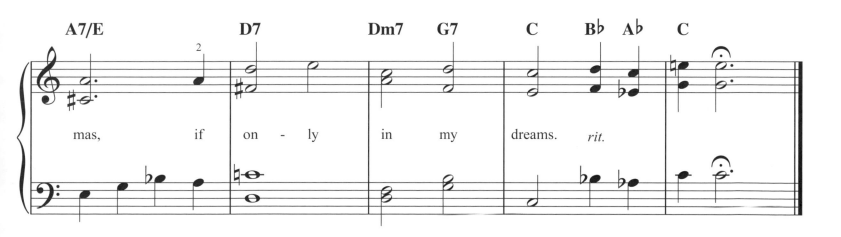

# IT'S BEGINNING TO LOOK LIKE CHRISTMAS

By MEREDITH WILLSON

gin-ning to look a lot like Christ - mas, toys in ev - 'ry

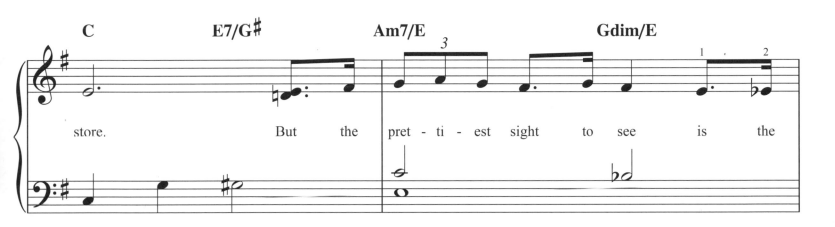

store. But the pret - ti - est sight to see is the

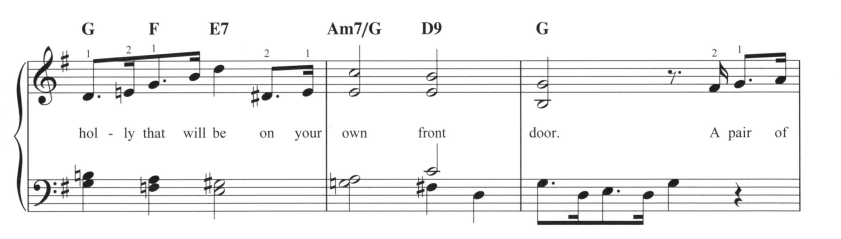

hol - ly that will be on your own front door. A pair of

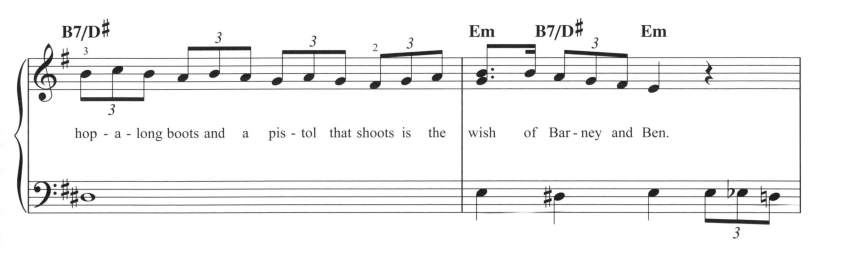

hop - a - long boots and a pis - tol that shoots is the wish of Bar - ney and Ben.

74

Dolls that will talk and will go for a walk is the hope of Jan-ice and Jen. And

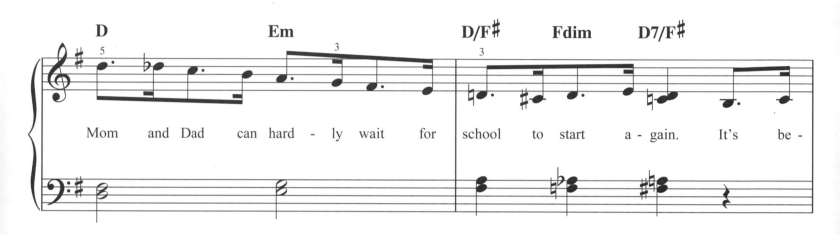

Mom and Dad can hard-ly wait for school to start a-gain. It's be-

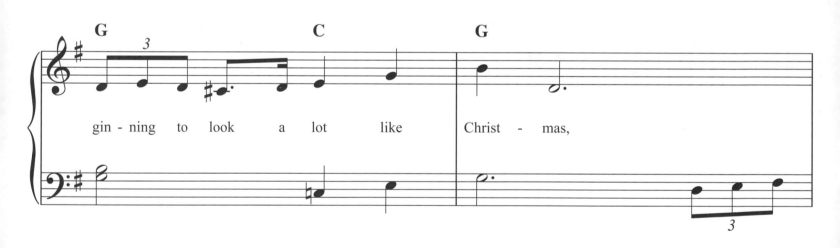

gin-ning to look a lot like Christ-mas,

ev-'ry-where you go. There's a tree in the Grand Ho-tel,

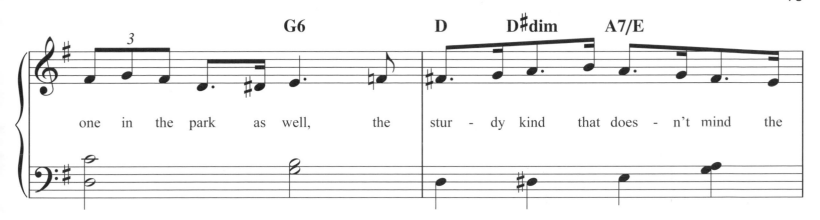

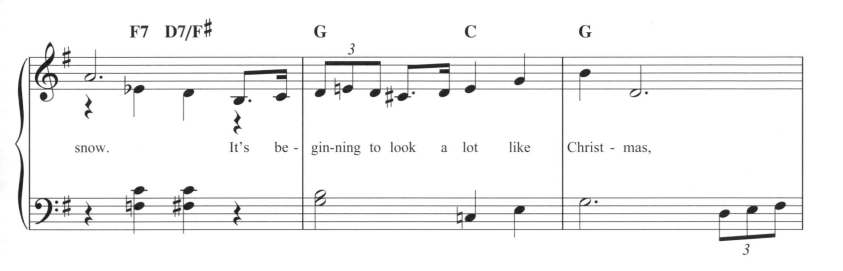

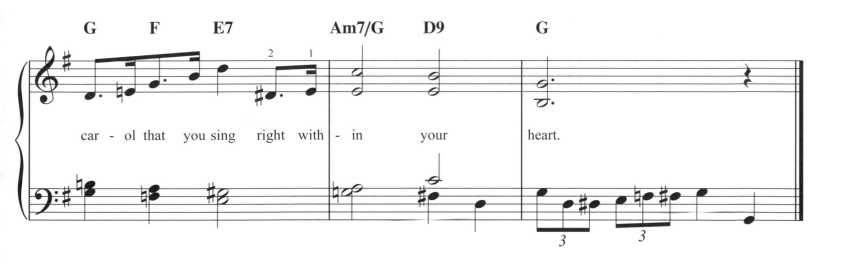

# JINGLE BELL ROCK

Words and Music by JOE BEAL
and JIM BOOTHE

now the jin - gle hop has be - gun. ___ in the frost - y

air. What a bright time, ___ it's the right time ___ to

rock the night a - way. Jin - gle bell time ___ is a

swell time ___ to go glid - in' in a one-horse sleigh. ___

Gid - dy - ap, jin - gle horse, pick up your feet, ____

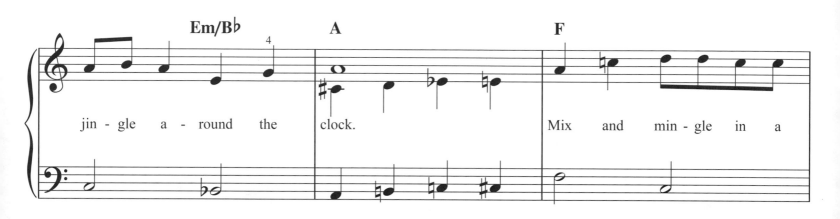

jin - gle a - round the clock. Mix and min - gle in a

jin - gl - in' beat, __ that's the jin - gle bell, that's the jin - gle bell,

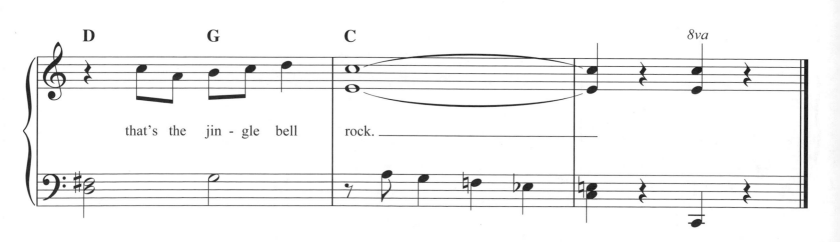

that's the jin - gle bell rock. ____

# PRETTY PAPER

Words and Music by
WILLIE NELSON

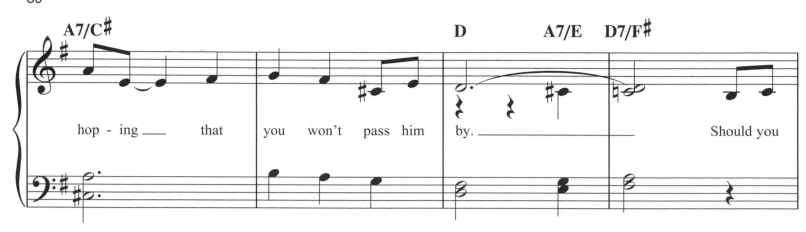

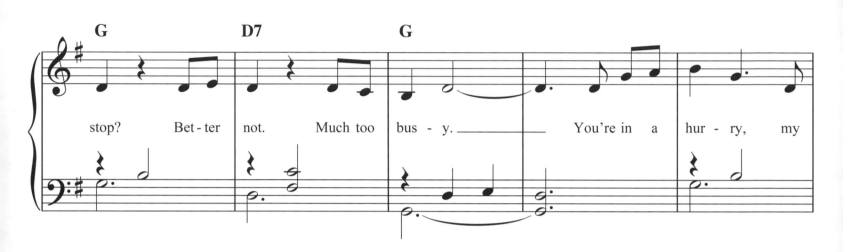

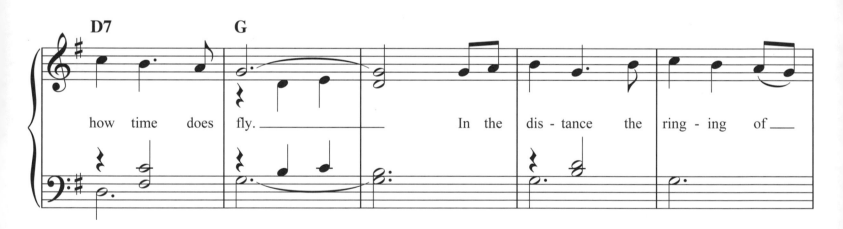

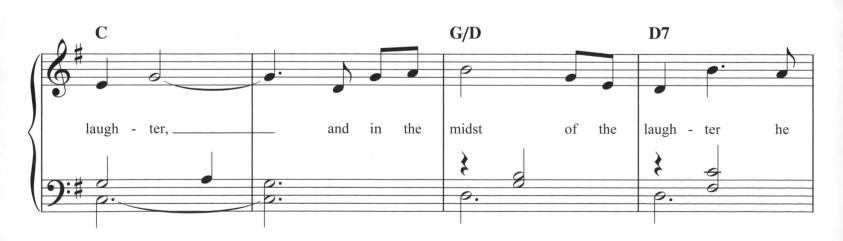

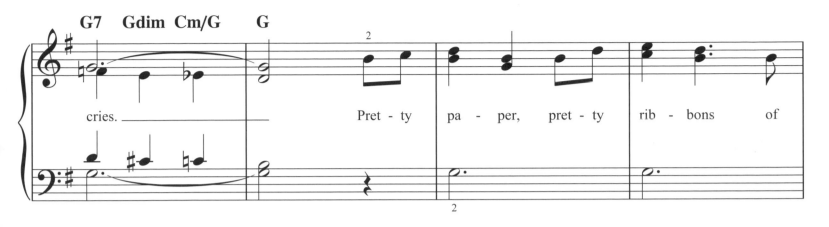

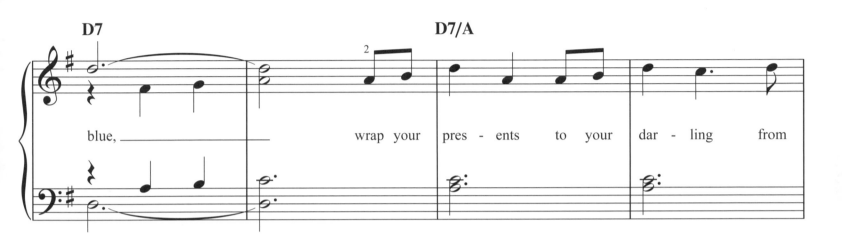

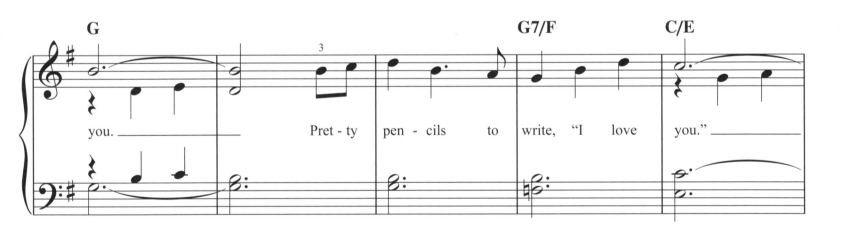

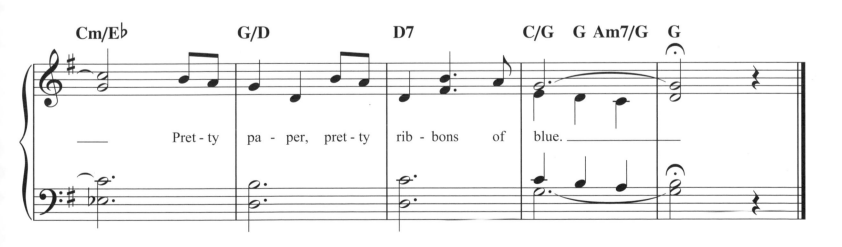

# LET IT SNOW! LET IT SNOW! LET IT SNOW!

Words by SAMMY CAHN
Music by JULE STYNE

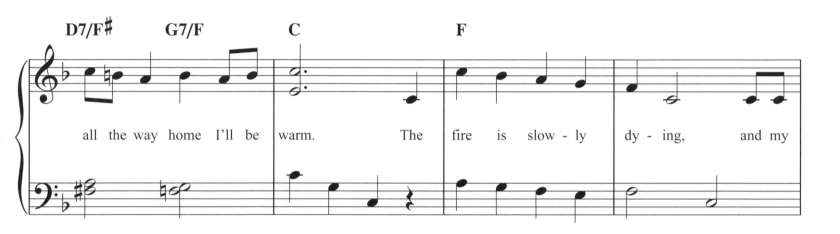

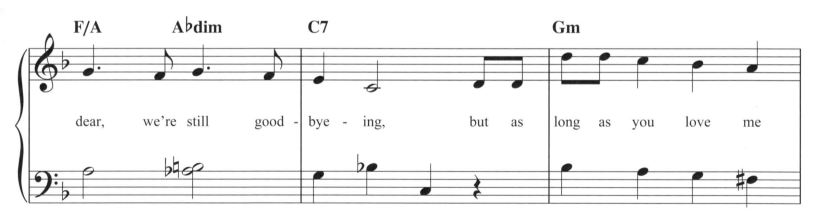

# THE LITTLE DRUMMER BOY

Words and Music by HARRY SIMEONE,
HENRY ONORATI and KATHERINE DAVIS

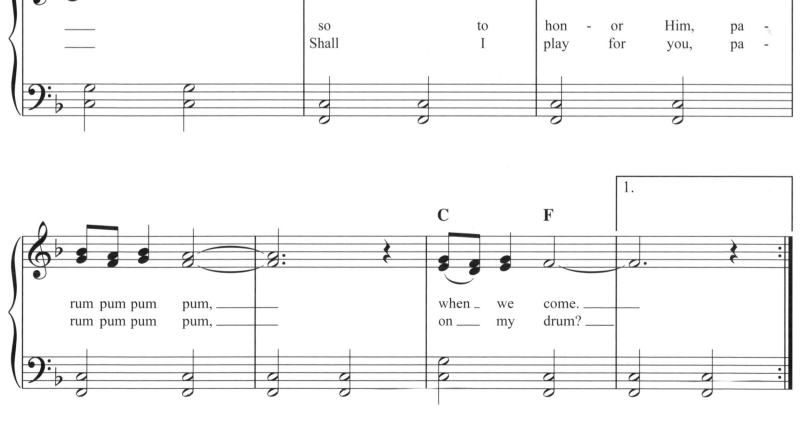

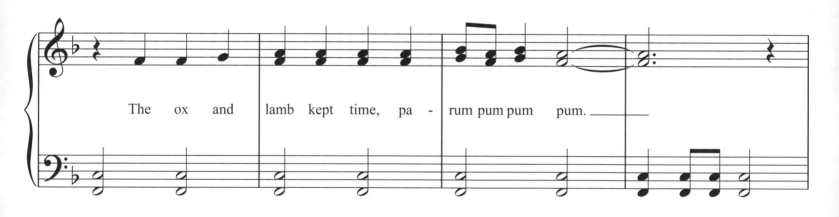

# LITTLE SAINT NICK

Words and Music by BRIAN WILSON
and MIKE LOVE

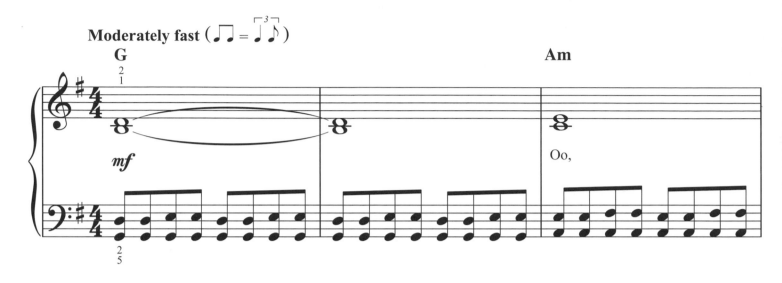

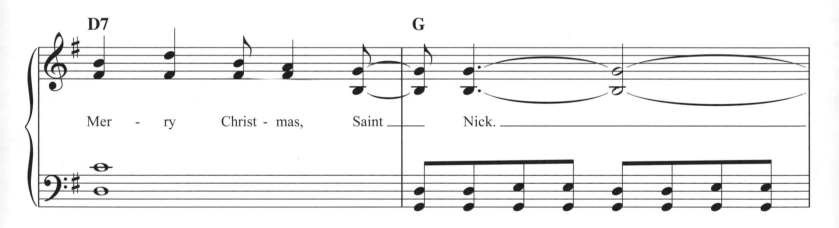

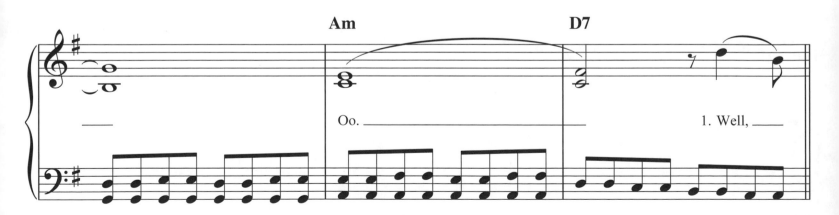

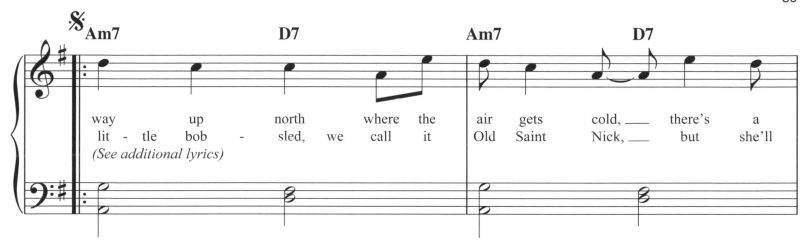

way      up      north      where the      air   gets      cold, ___      there's      a
lit - tle   bob - sled,   we   call   it      Old   Saint      Nick, ___      but      she'll
*(See additional lyrics)*

tale   a - bout   Christ - mas   that   you've      all   been      told. ___   And      a
walk   a   to - bog - gan   with   a      four - speed      stick. ___      She's

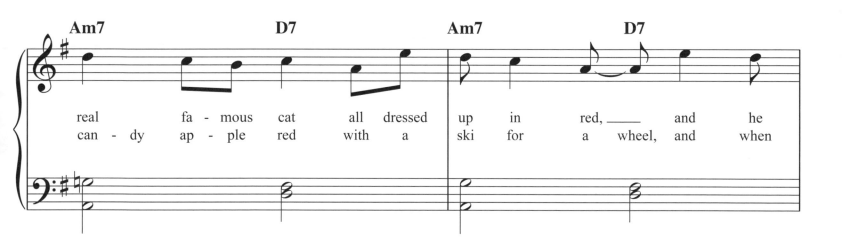

real      fa - mous   cat      all   dressed      up   in      red, ___      and      he
can - dy   ap - ple   red   with   a      ski   for      a   wheel,   and      when

spends the   whole _ year   work - in'      out   on his   sled. _ } It's      the      Lit - tle   Saint   Nick. (Lit - tle
San - ta   hits   the   gas,   man, just      watch her ___   peel. _

90

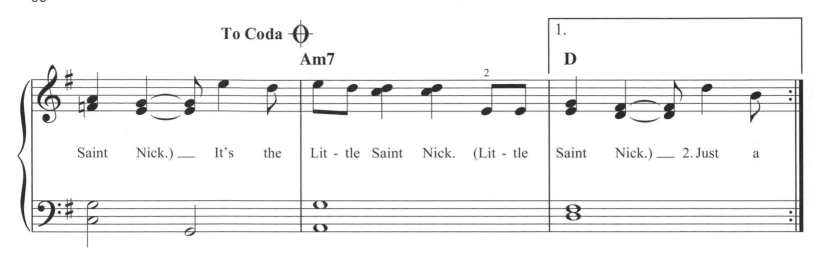

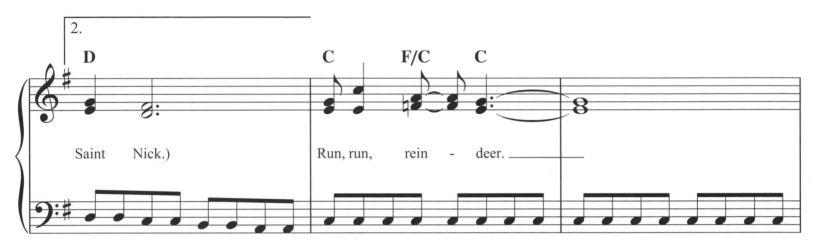

CODA

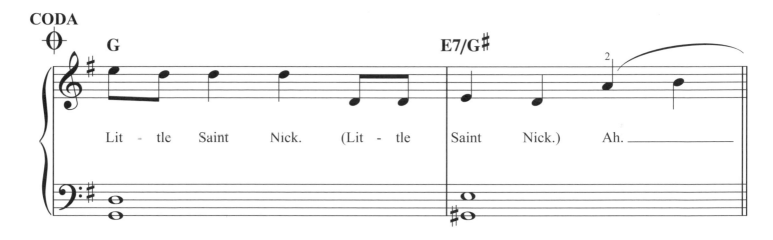

Lit - tle Saint Nick. (Lit - tle Saint Nick.) Ah. _____

_____ Mer - ry Christ - mas, Saint _____ Nick. _____

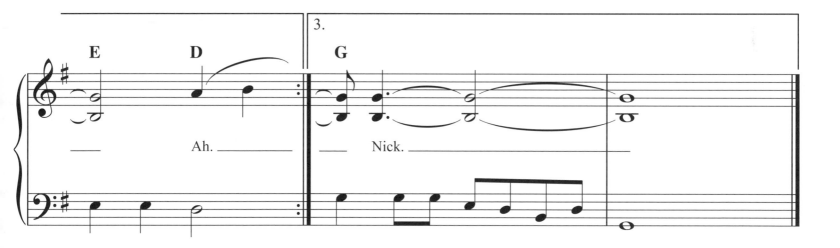

_____ Ah. _____ _____ Nick. _____

*Additional Lyrics*

3. And haulin' through the snow at a fright'nin' speed,
   With half a dozen deer with Rudy to lead,
   He's gotta wear his goggles 'cause the snow really flies,
   And he's cruisin' ev'ry pad with a little surprise.

# A MARSHMALLOW WORLD

Words by CARL SIGMAN
Music by PETER DE ROSE

ev - er it snows. The world is your snow - ball; just for a song, get out and roll it a -

long. It's a yum, yum - my world made for sweet - hearts; \_\_\_\_ take a

walk with your fa - vor - ite girl. It's a sug - ar date; what if

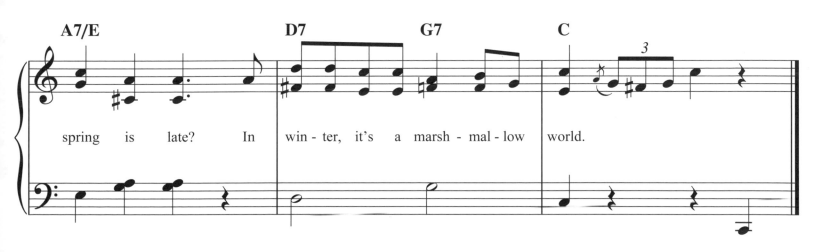

spring is late? In win - ter, it's a marsh - mal - low world.

# MARY, DID YOU KNOW?

Words and Music by MARK LOWRY
and BUDDY GREENE

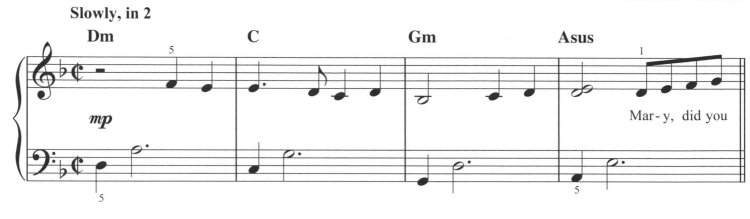

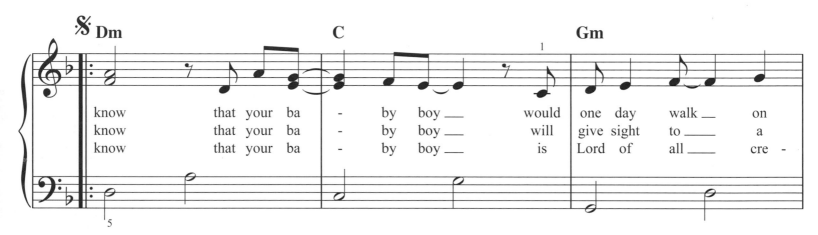

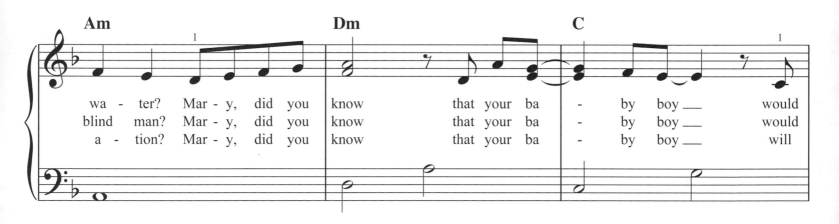

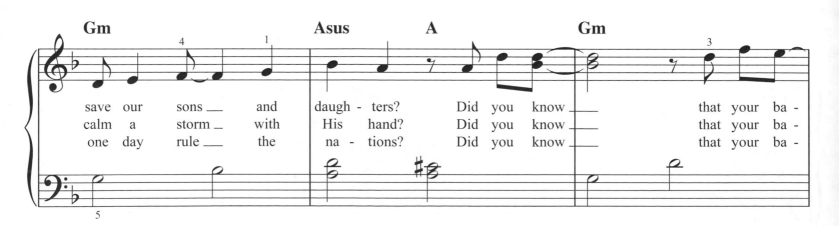

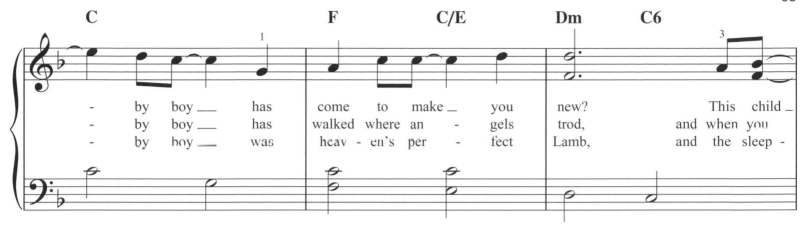

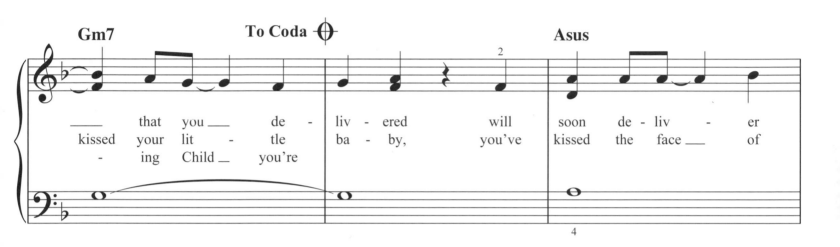

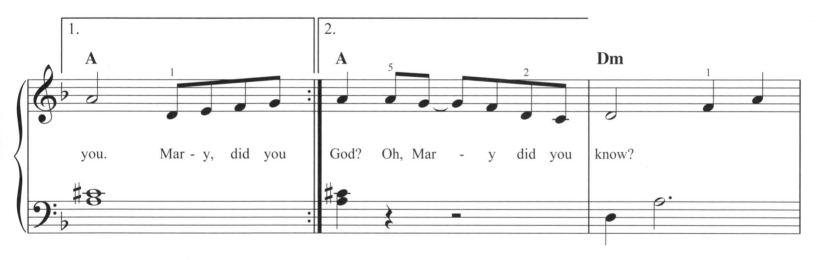

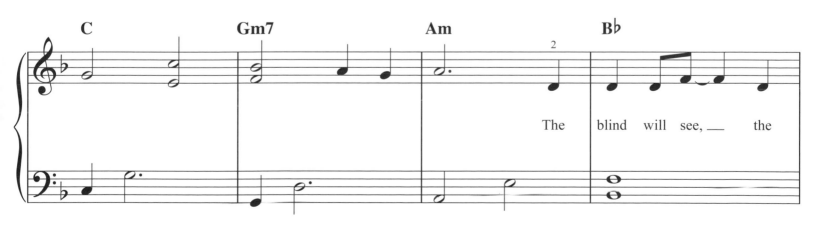

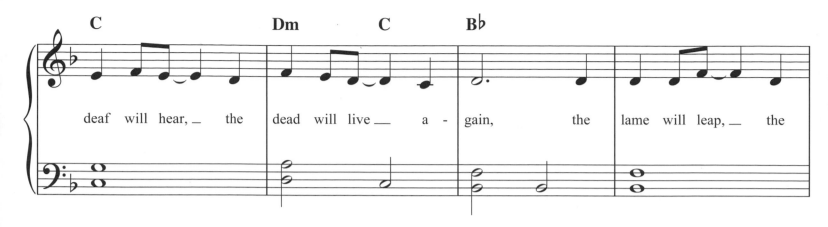

deaf will hear, __ the dead will live __ a - gain, the lame will leap, __ the

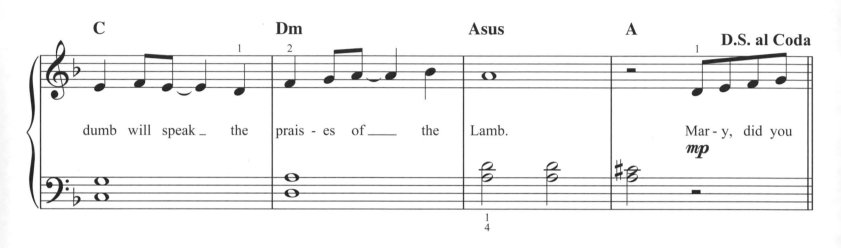

dumb will speak __ the prais - es of __ the Lamb. Mar - y, did you

**CODA**

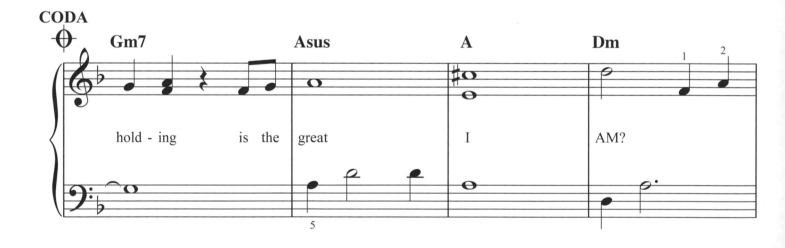

hold - ing is the great I AM?

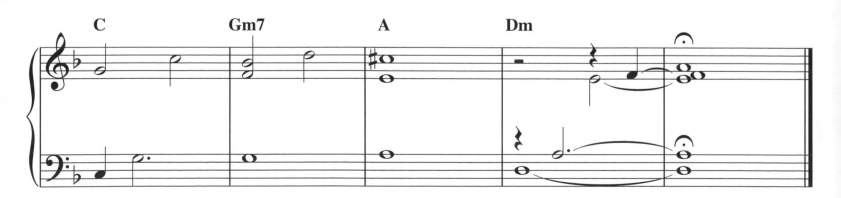

# ROCKIN' AROUND THE CHRISTMAS TREE

Music and Lyrics by
JOHNNY MARKS

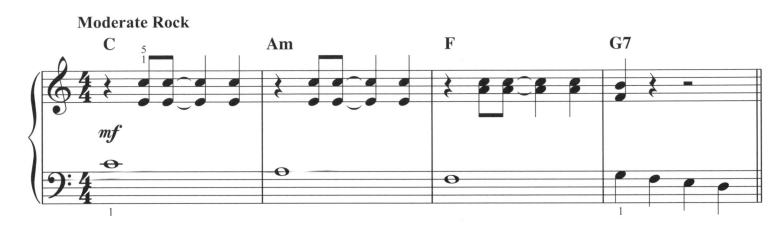

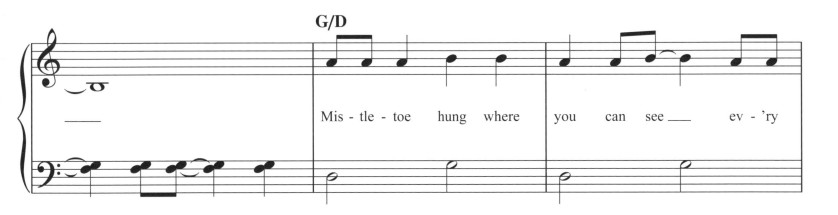

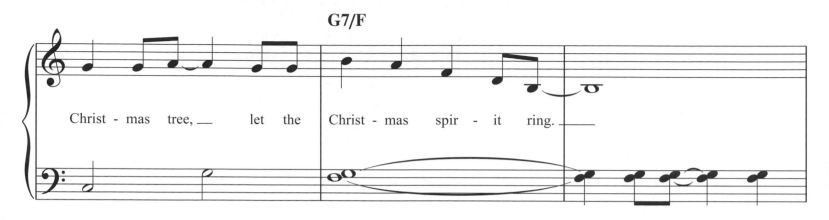

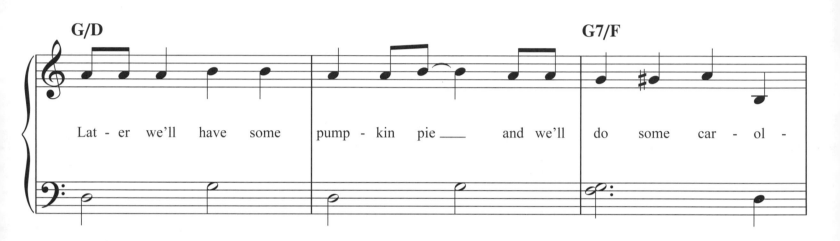

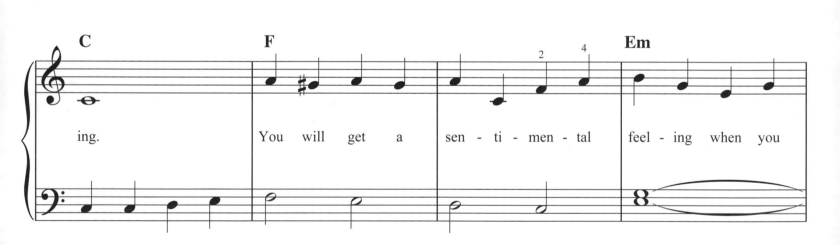

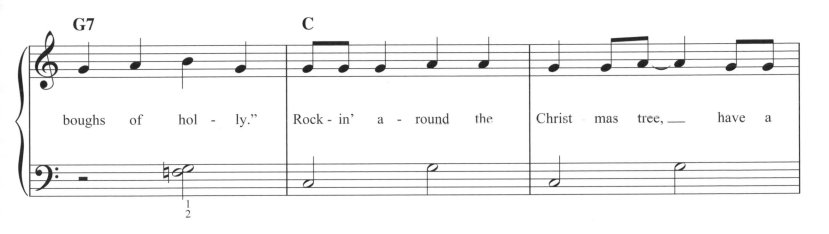

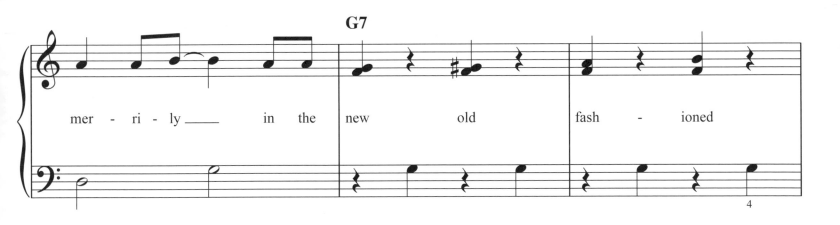

# MERRY CHRISTMAS, DARLING

Words and Music by RICHARD CARPENTER
and FRANK POOLER

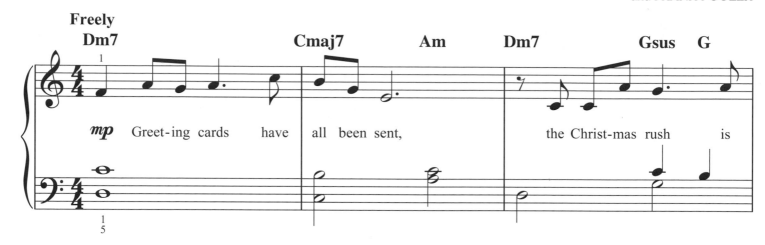

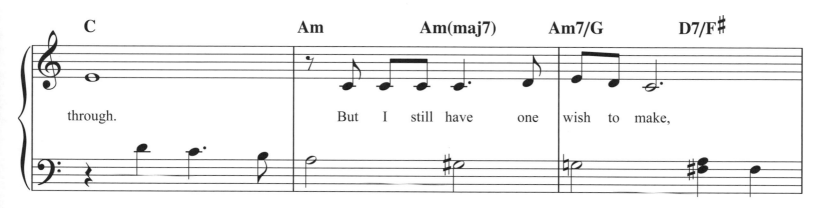

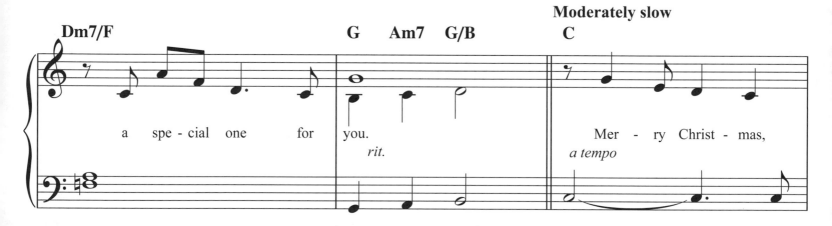

I can dream and, in my dreams, I'm Christ-mas - ing with

you. The hol - i - days are joy - ful.

There's al - ways some-thing new. But ____ ev - 'ry - day's a

hol - i - day when I'm near to you. All the

lights on my tree      I wish you could see,      I wish it ev - 'ry day. —

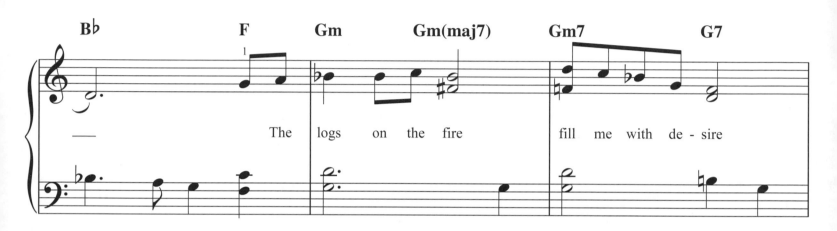

— The logs on the fire      fill me with de - sire

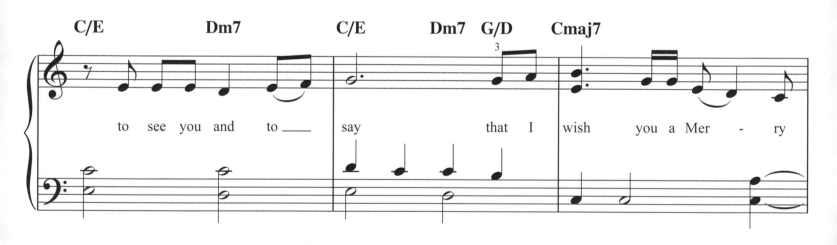

to see you and to ____ say      that I wish you a Mer - ry

Christ - mas.      Hap - py New Year,    too.

# MISTLETOE AND HOLLY

Words and Music by FRANK SINATRA,
DOK STANFORD and HENRY W. SANICOLA

know. Then comes that big night; giv-ing the tree the

trim. You'll hear voic-es by star-light sing-ing a yule-tide

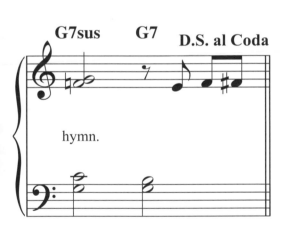

hymn.

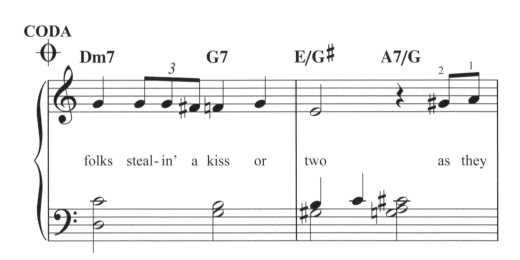

folks steal-in' a kiss or two as they

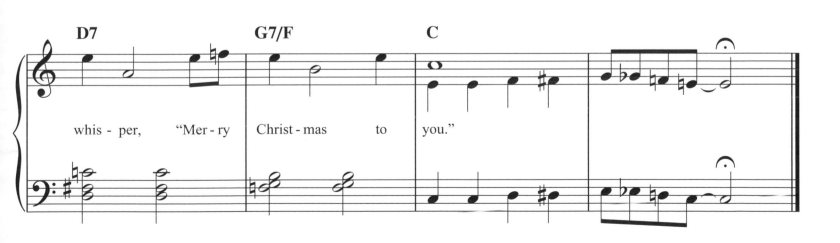

whis-per, "Mer-ry Christ-mas to you."

# THE MOST WONDERFUL TIME OF THE YEAR

Words and Music by EDDIE POLA
and GEORGE WYLE

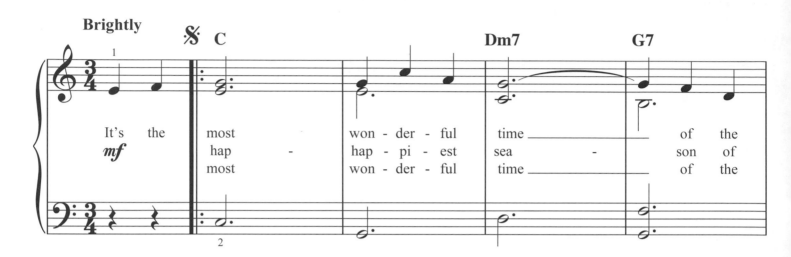

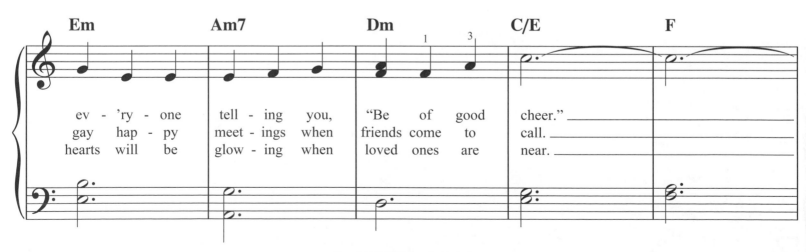

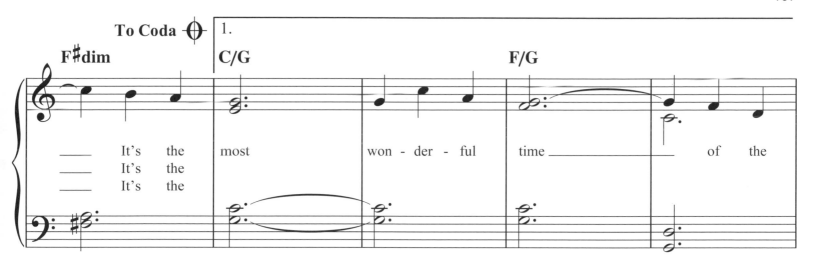

**To Coda** ⊕ | 1.

F#dim | C/G | | F/G

\_\_\_\_ It's the most won - der - ful time _____ of the
\_\_\_\_ It's the
\_\_\_\_ It's the

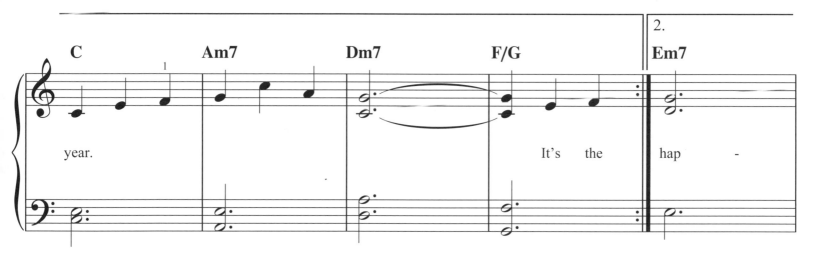

C | Am7 | Dm7 | F/G | 2. Em7

year. It's the hap -

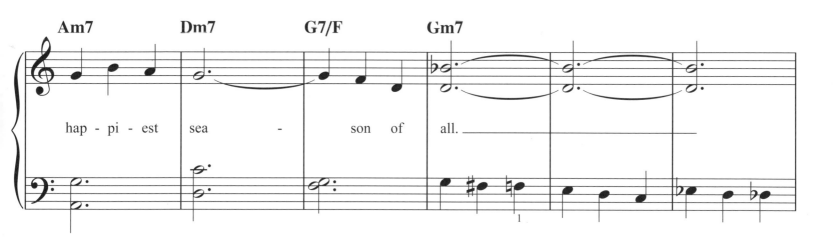

Am7 | Dm7 | G7/F | Gm7

hap - pi - est sea - son of all. \_\_\_\_\_

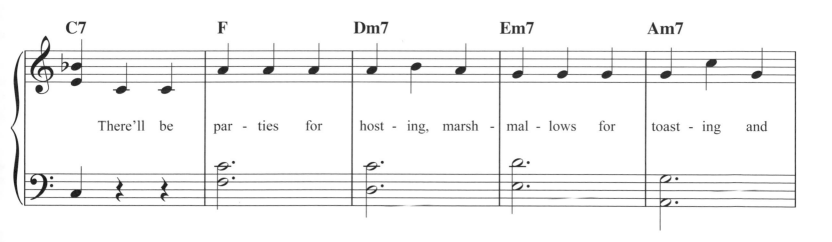

C7 | F | Dm7 | Em7 | Am7

There'll be par - ties for host - ing, marsh - mal - lows for toast - ing and

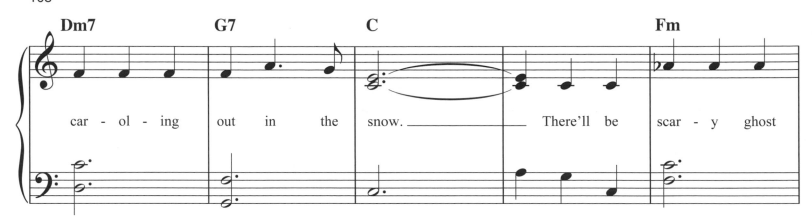

car - ol - ing    out    in    the    snow. _____    There'll    be    scar - y    ghost

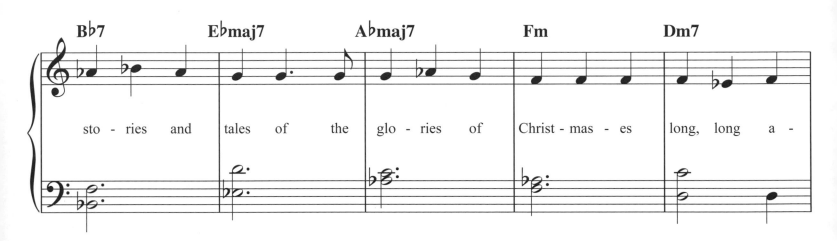

sto - ries    and    tales    of    the    glo - ries    of    Christ - mas - es    long,    long    a -

go. _____    It's    the

**CODA**

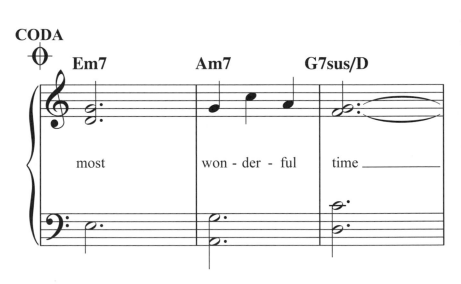

most    won - der - ful    time _____

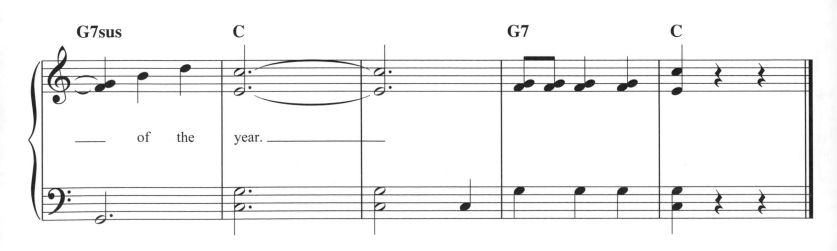

_____    of    the    year. _____

# SANTA BABY

By JOAN JAVITS,
PHIL SPRINGER and TONY SPRINGER

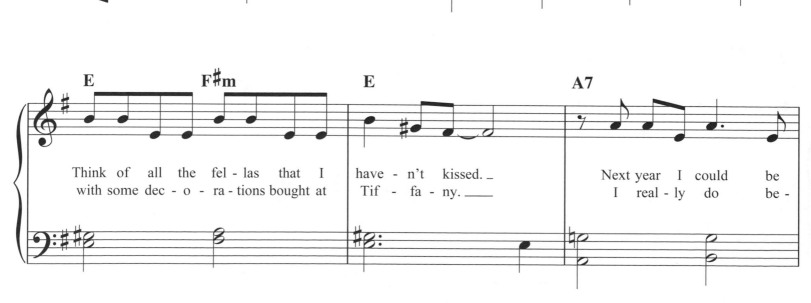

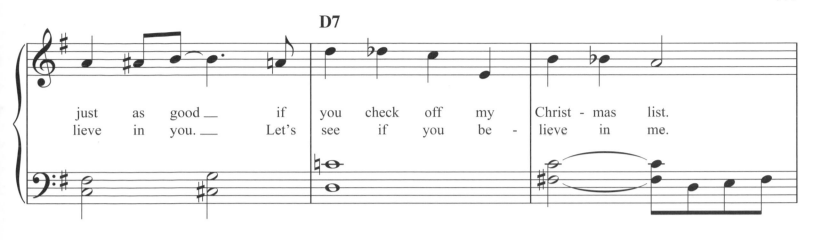

just as good ___ if you check off my Christ - mas list.
lieve in you. ___ Let's see if you be - lieve in me.

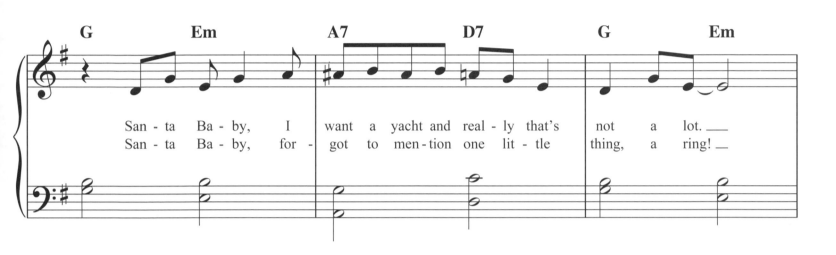

San - ta Ba - by, I want a yacht and real - ly that's not a lot. ___
San - ta Ba - by, for - got to men - tion one lit - tle thing, a ring! ___

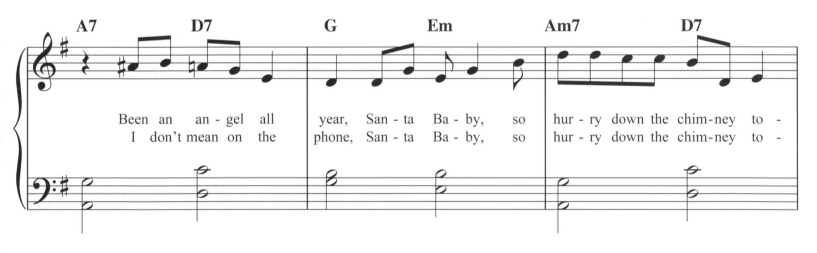

Been an an - gel all year, San - ta Ba - by, so hur - ry down the chim - ney to -
I don't mean on the phone, San - ta Ba - by, so hur - ry down the chim - ney to -

night.

night.

# MY FAVORITE THINGS

## from THE SOUND OF MUSIC

Lyrics by OSCAR HAMMERSTEIN II
Music by RICHARD RODGERS

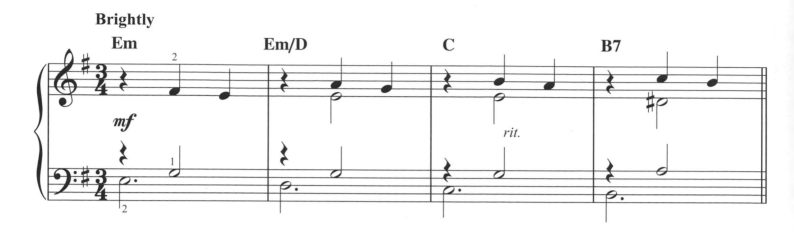

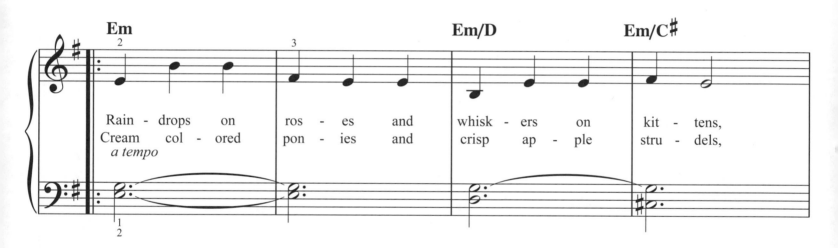

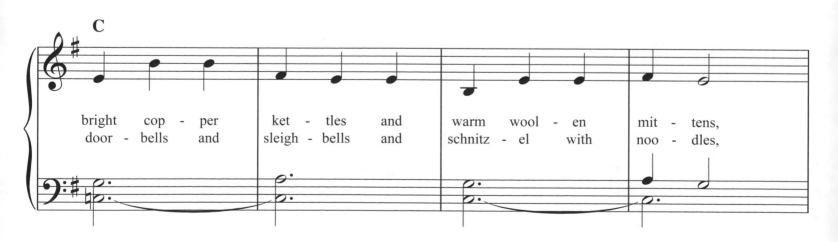

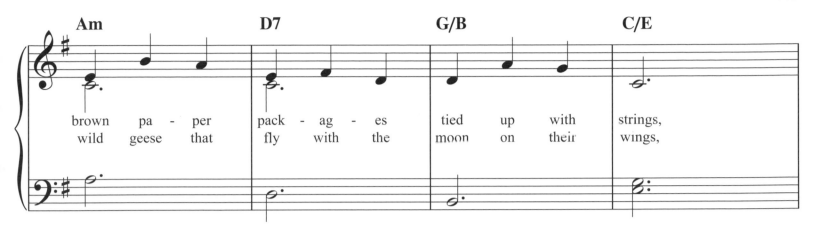

Am  D7  G/B  C/E

brown pa - per pack - ag - es tied up with strings,
wild geese that fly with the moon on their wings,

G/D  C  F#m7♭5  B7

these are a few of my fa - vor - ite things.
these are a few of my fa - vor - ite things.

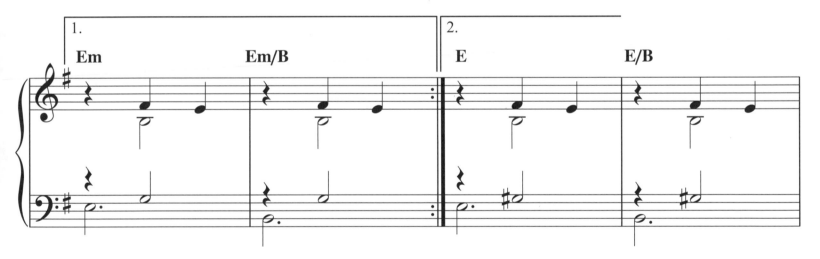

1.  2.
Em  Em/B  E  E/B

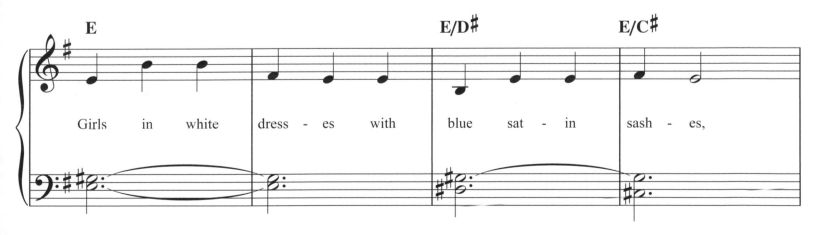

E  E/D#  E/C#

Girls in white dress - es with blue sat - in sash - es,

snow - flakes that stay on my nose and eye - lash - es,

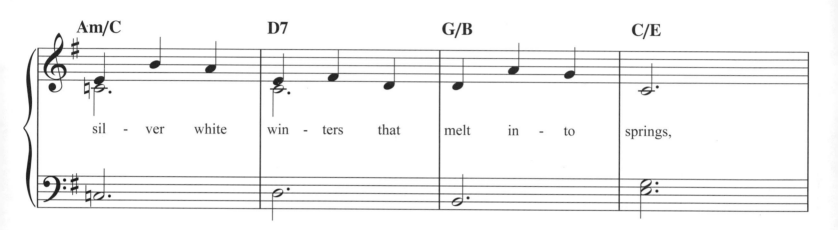

sil - ver white win - ters that melt in - to springs,

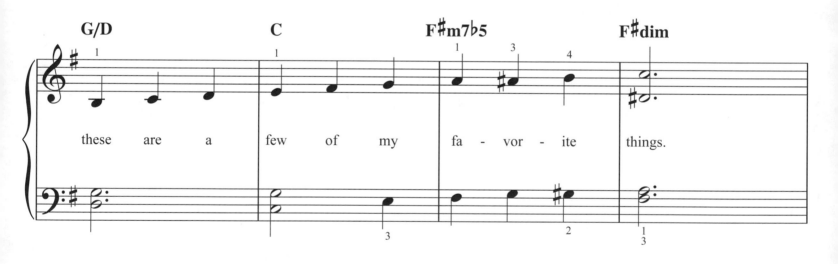

these are a few of my fa - vor - ite things.

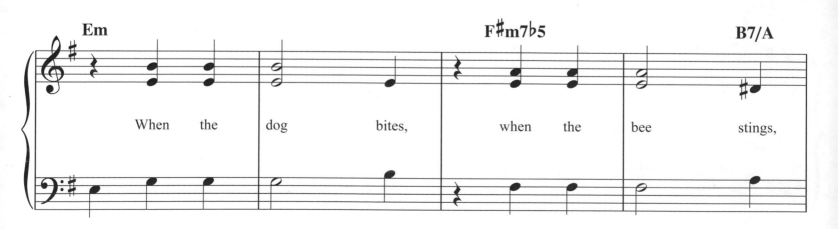

When the dog bites, when the bee stings,

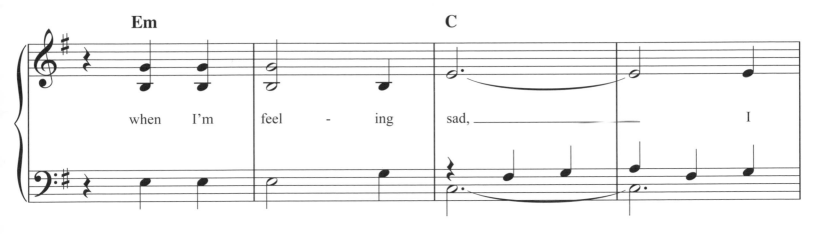

when I'm feel - ing sad, _____ I

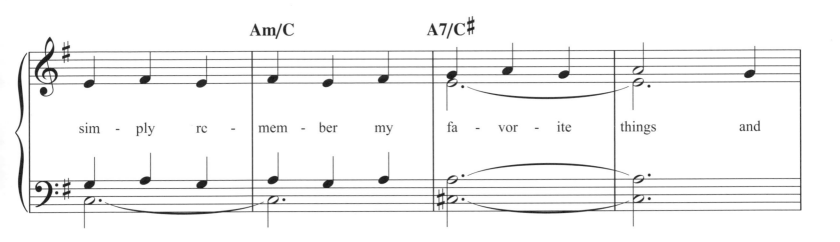

sim - ply re - mem - ber my fa - vor - ite things and

then I don't feel so

bad.

# NUTTIN' FOR CHRISTMAS

Words and Music by SID TEPPER
and ROY C. BENNETT

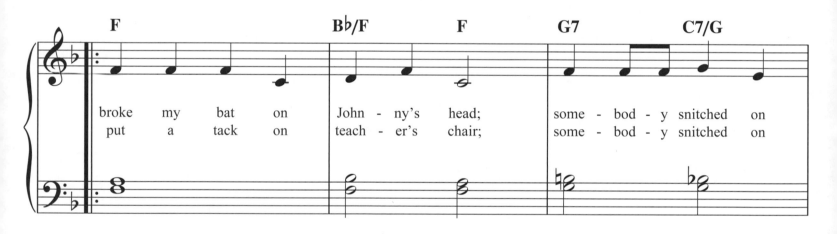

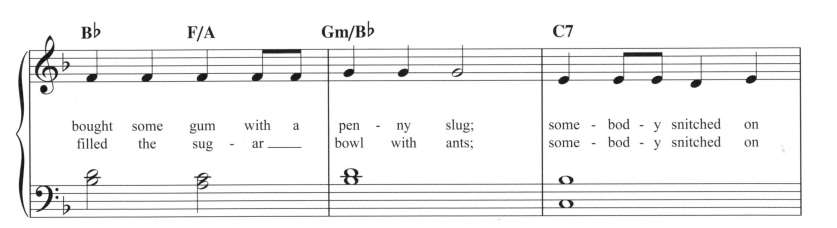

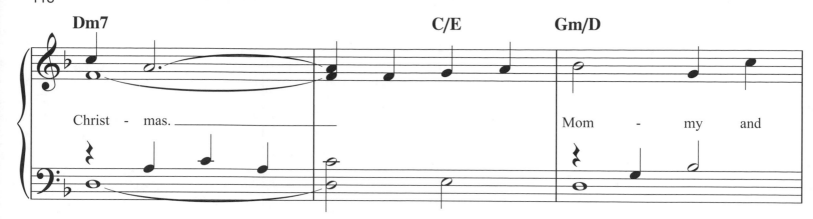

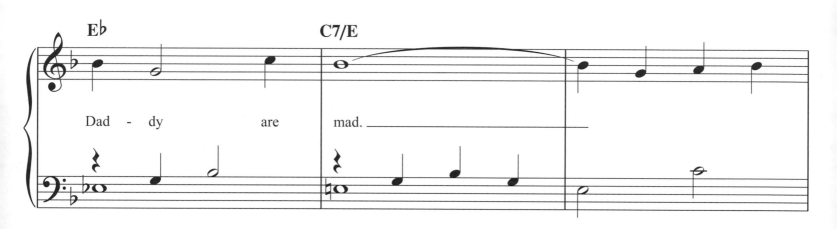

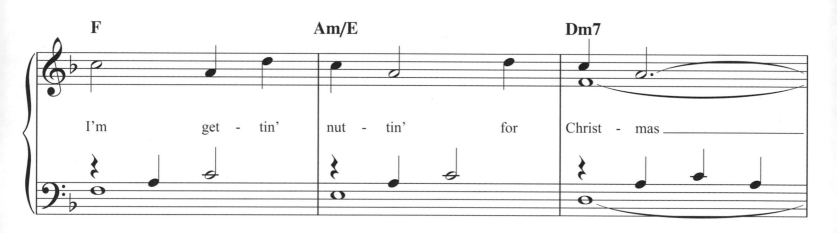

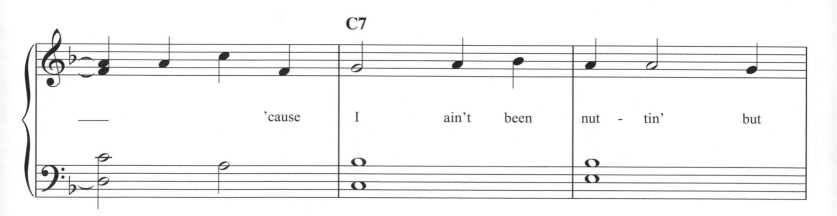

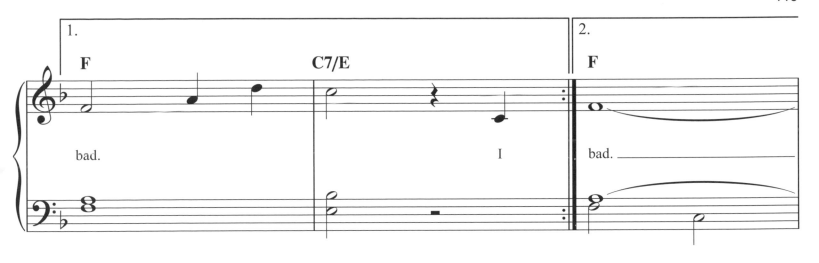

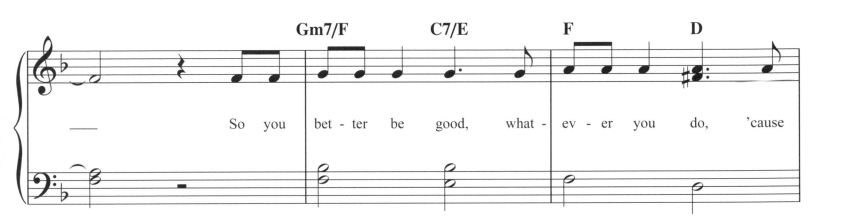

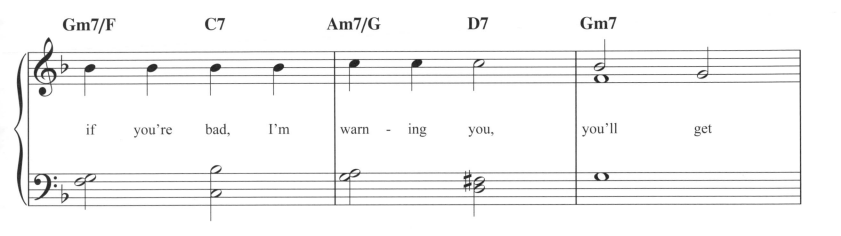

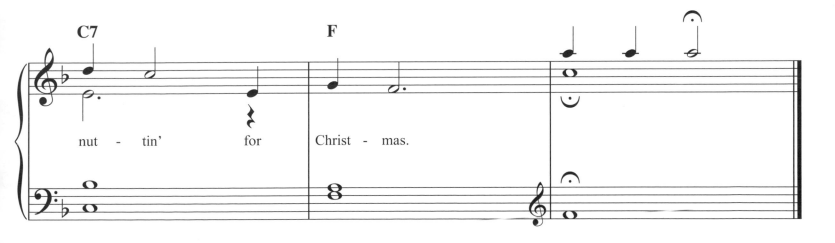

# RUDOLPH THE RED-NOSED REINDEER

Music and Lyrics by
JOHNNY MARKS

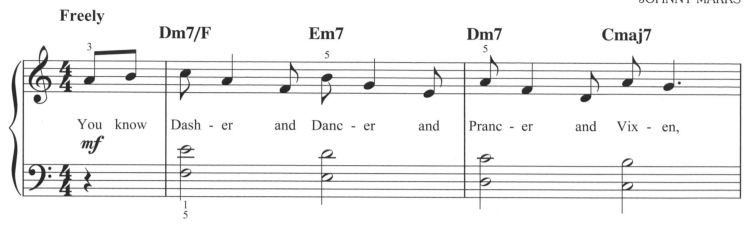

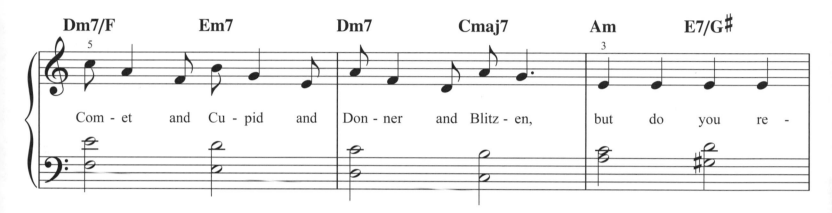

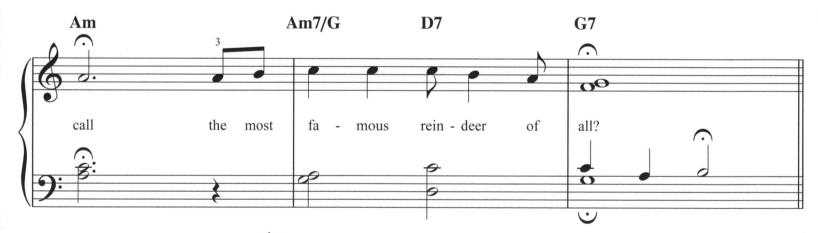

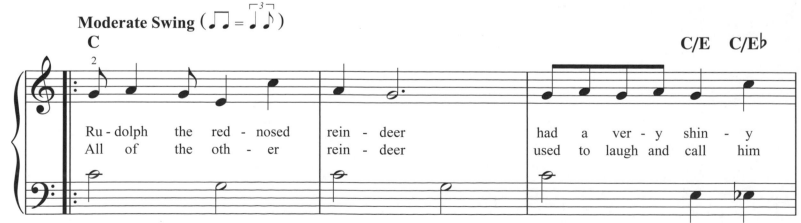

121

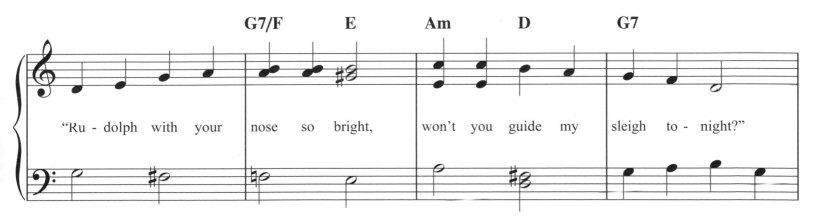

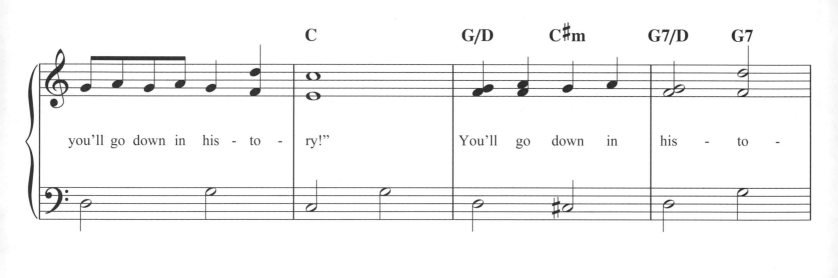

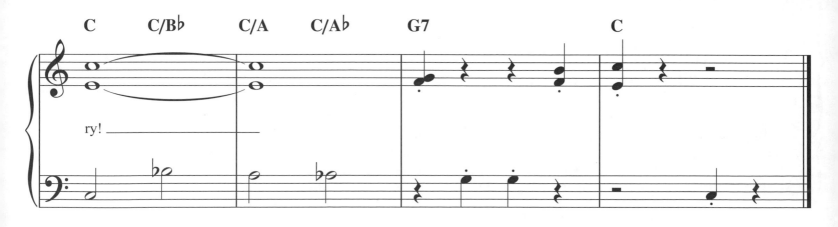

# SANTA CLAUS IS COMIN' TO TOWN

Words by HAVEN GILLESPIE
Music by J. FRED COOTS

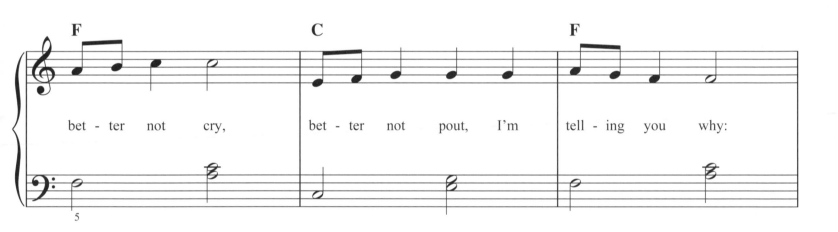

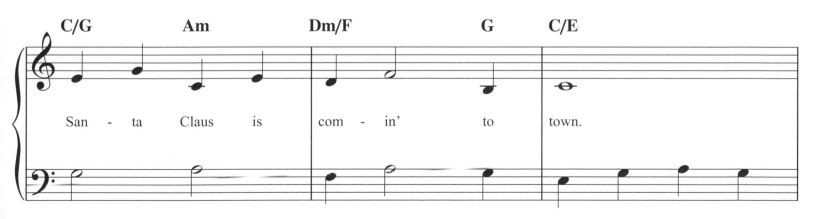

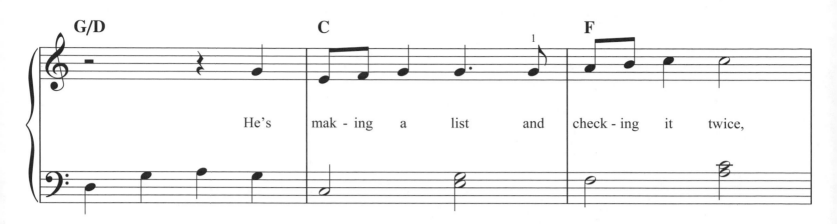

He's mak-ing a list and check-ing it twice,

gon-na find out who's naugh-ty and nice, San-ta Claus is

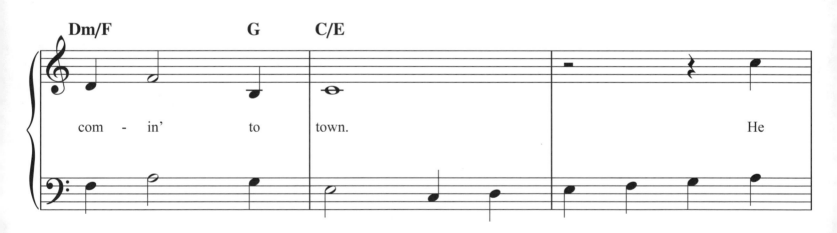

com-in' to town. He

sees you when you're sleep-in', he knows when you're a-

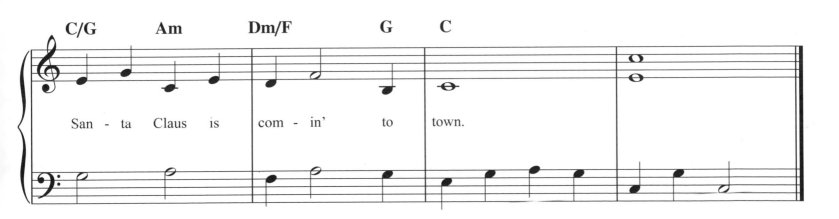

# SILVER AND GOLD

Music and Lyrics by
JOHNNY MARKS

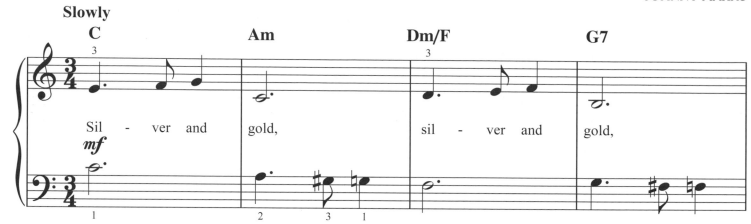

Silver and gold, sil - ver and gold,

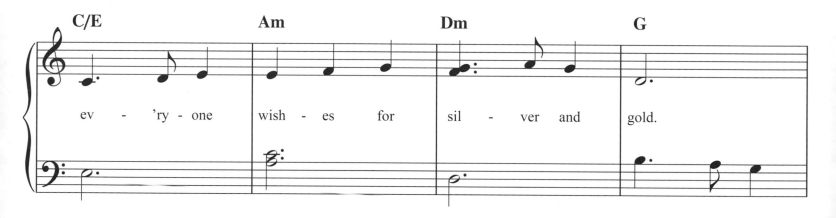

ev - 'ry - one wish - es for sil - ver and gold.

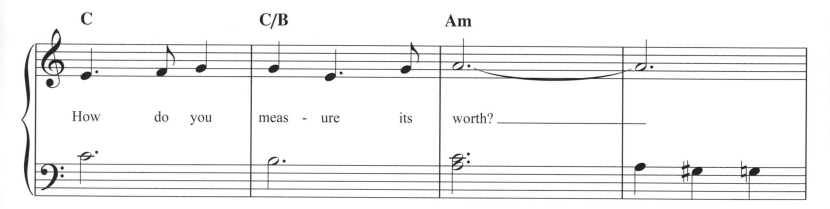

How do you meas - ure its worth? _____

Just by the pleas - ure it gives here on earth.

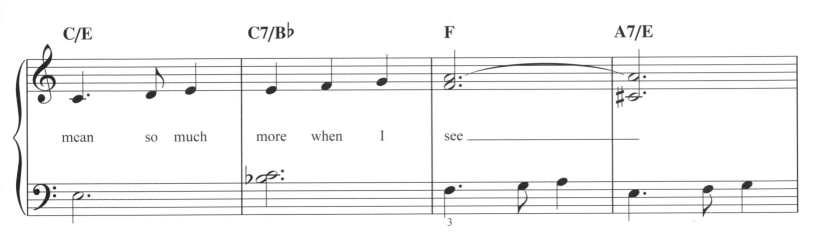

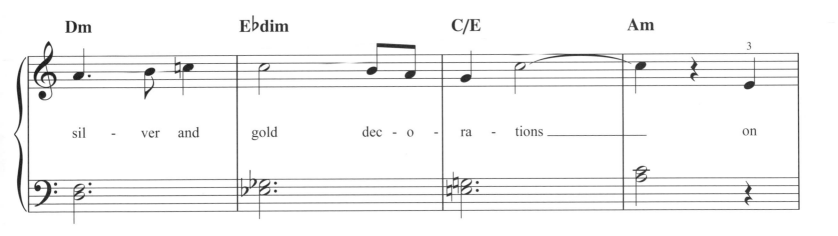

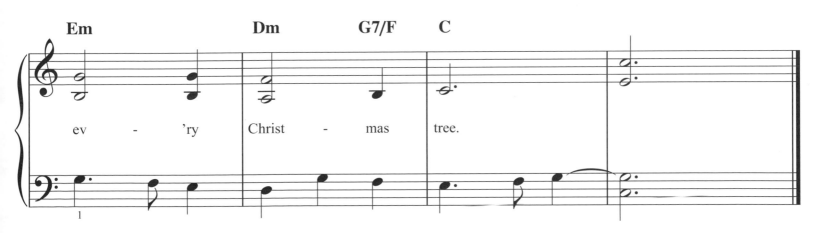

# SLEIGH RIDE

Music by LEROY ANDERSON
Words by MITCHELL PARISH

Just hear those

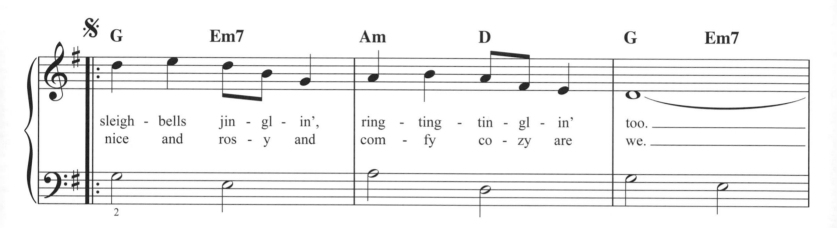

sleigh - bells jin - gl - in', ring - ting - tin - gl - in' too. ____
nice and ros - y and com - fy co - zy are we. ____

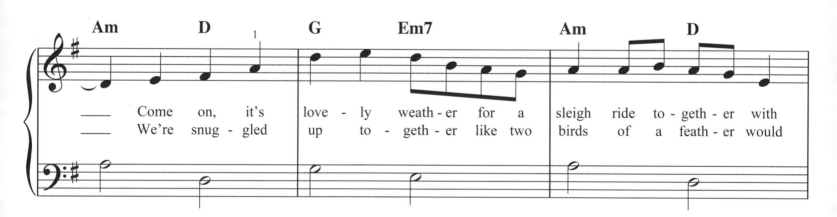

____ Come on, it's love - ly weath - er for a sleigh ride to - geth - er with
____ We're snug - gled up to - geth - er like two birds of a feath - er would

you. ____ Out - side the snow is fall - in' and friends are call - in', "Yoo
be. ____ Let's take that road be - fore us and sing a cho - rus or

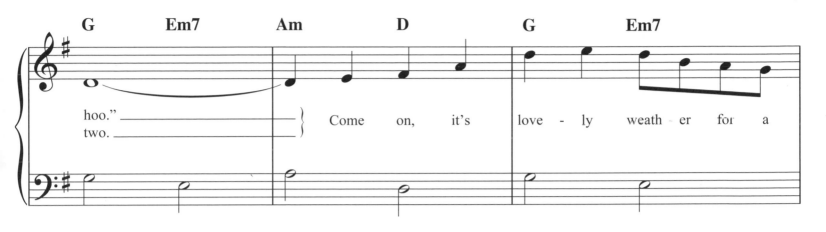

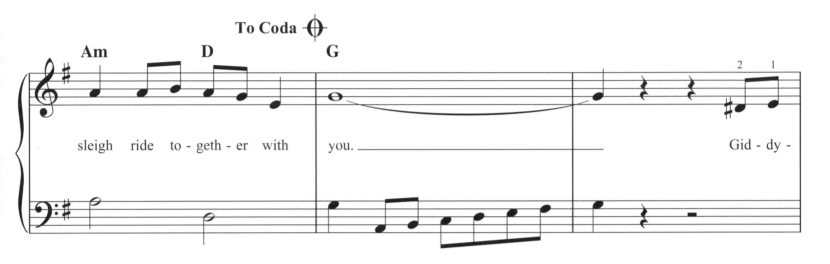

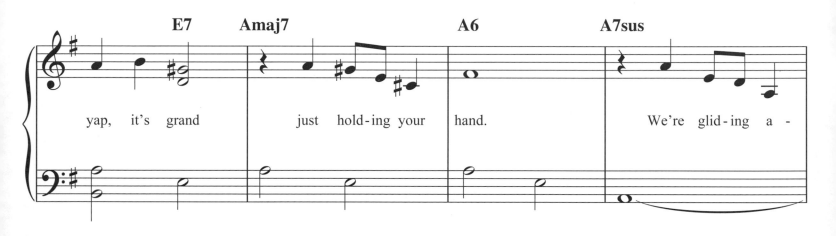

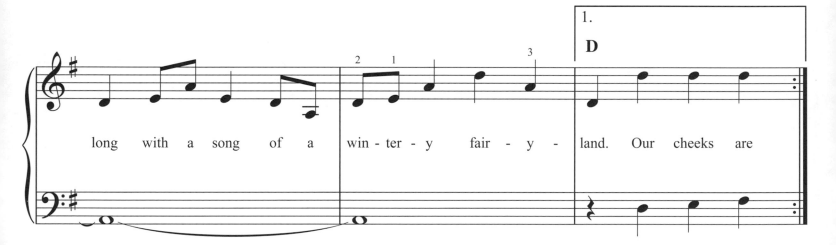

# SILVER BELLS
### from the Paramount Picture THE LEMON DROP KID

Words and Music by JAY LIVINGSTON
and RAY EVANS

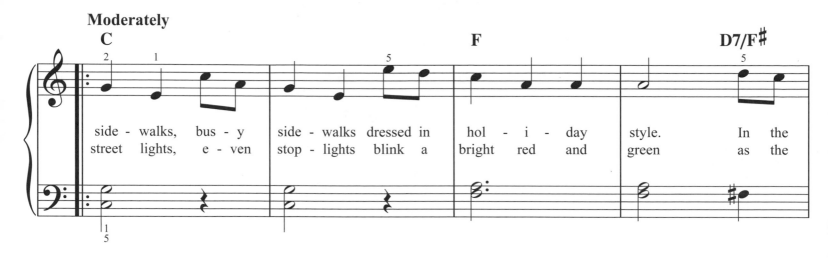

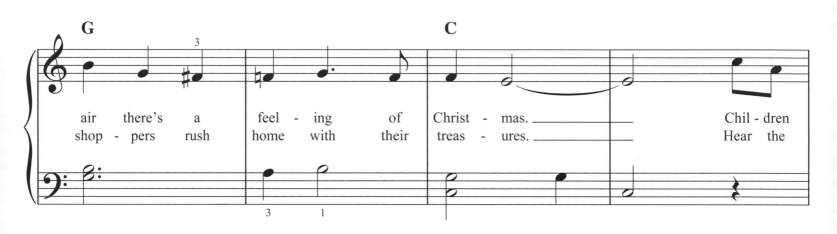

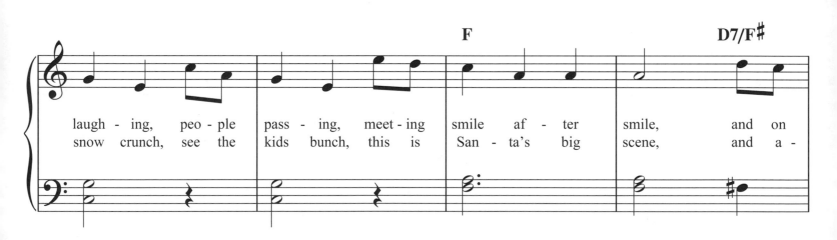

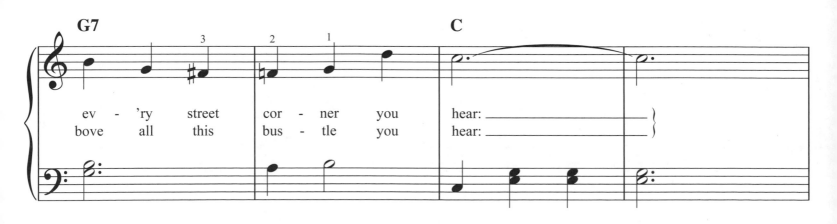

Sil - ver  bells,  sil - ver  bells,

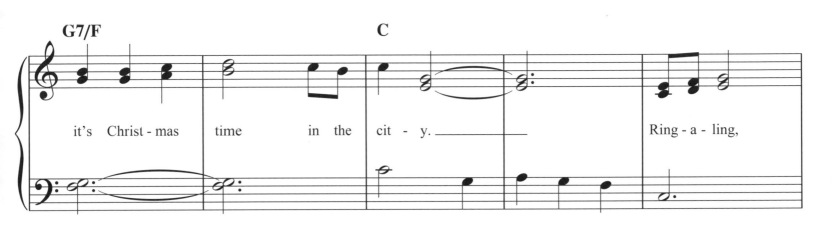

it's  Christ - mas  time  in  the  cit - y. _____  Ring - a - ling,

hear  them  ring,  soon  it  will

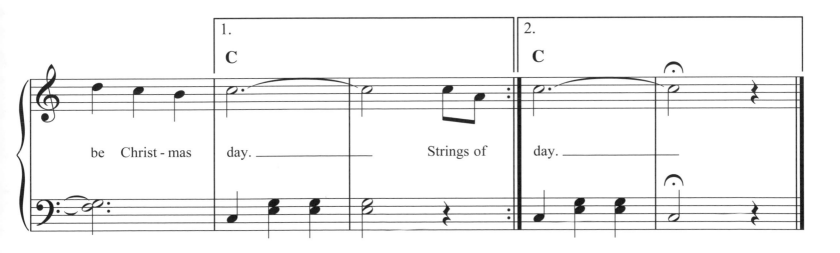

be  Christ - mas  day. _____  Strings of  day. _____

# Somewhere in My Memory

from the Twentieth Century Fox Motion Picture HOME ALONE

Words by LESLIE BRICUSSE
Music by JOHN WILLIAMS

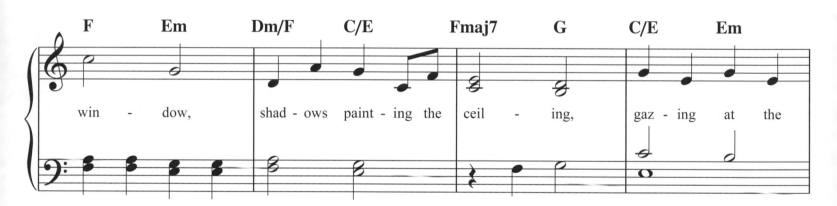

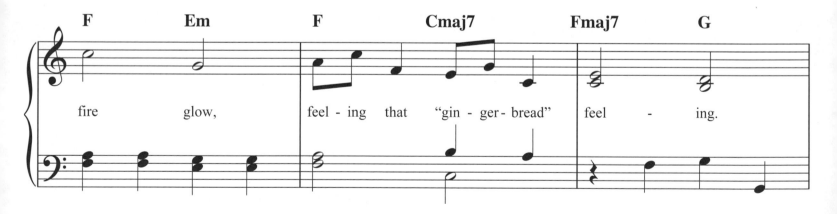

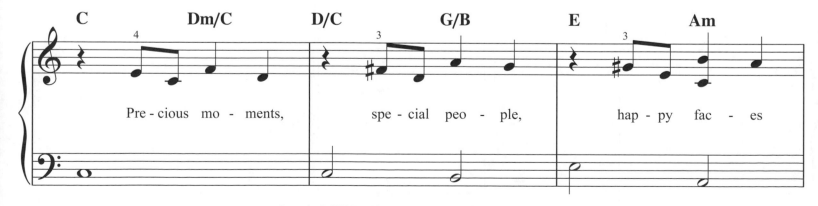

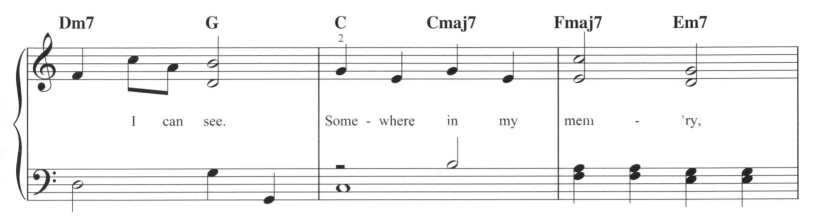

I can see. Some - where in my mem - 'ry,

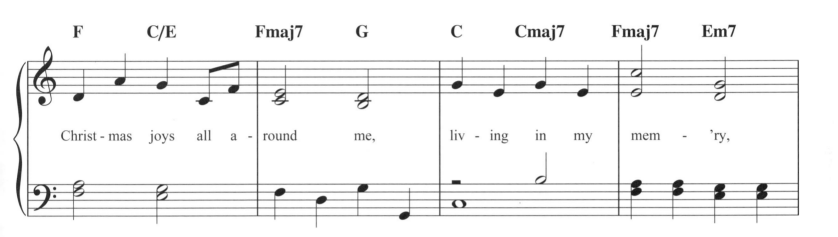

Christ - mas joys all a - round me, liv - ing in my mem - 'ry,

all of the mu - sic, all of the mag - ic, all of the fam - 'ly

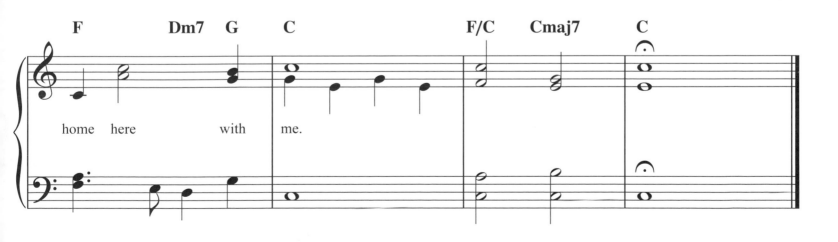

home here with me.

# THIS CHRISTMAS

Words and Music by DONNY HATHAWAY
and NADINE McKINNOR

137

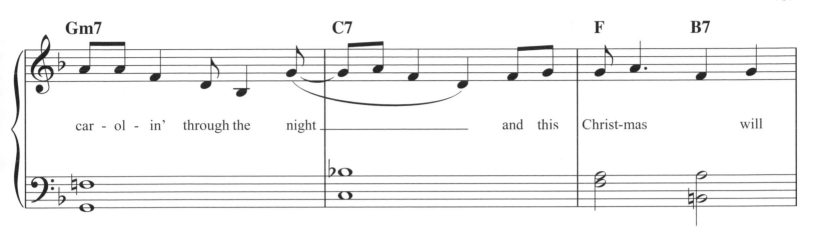

car - ol - in' through the night _____ and this Christ-mas will

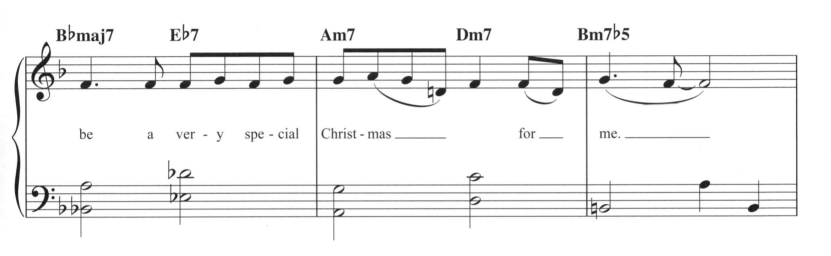

be a ver - y spe - cial Christ - mas _____ for ___ me. _____

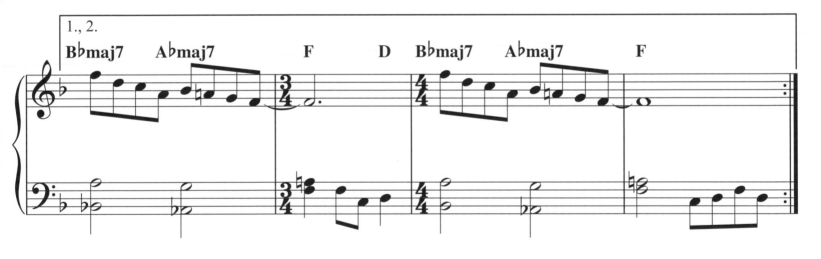

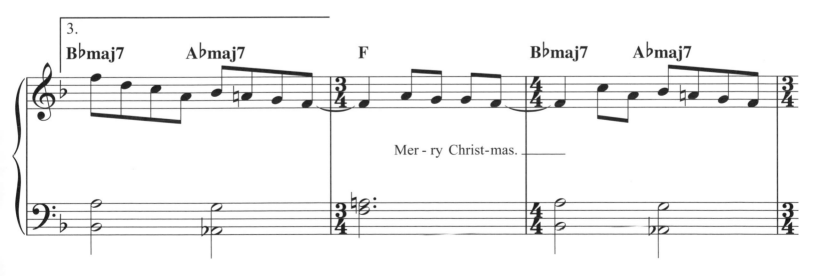

Mer - ry Christ-mas. _____

# WE NEED A LITTLE CHRISTMAS
## from MAME

Music and Lyric by
JERRY HERMAN

**Brightly**

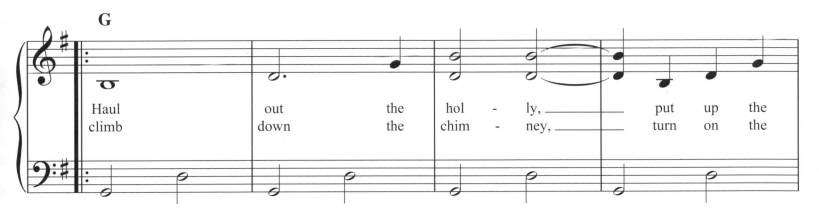

Haul out the hol - ly, ____ put up the
climb down the chim - ney, turn on the

tree be - fore my spir - it falls ____ a - gain.
bright - est string of lights I've ev - er seen.

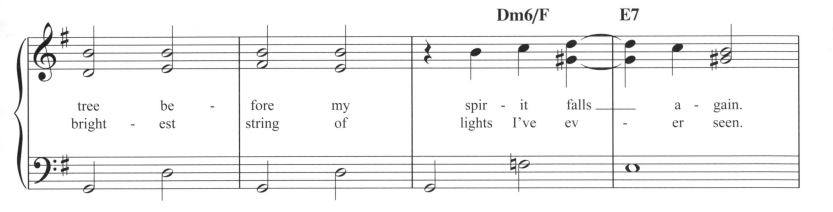

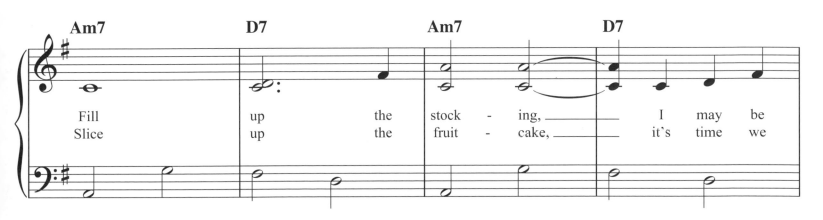

Fill up the stock - ing, ____ I may be
Slice up the fruit - cake, ____ it's time we

140

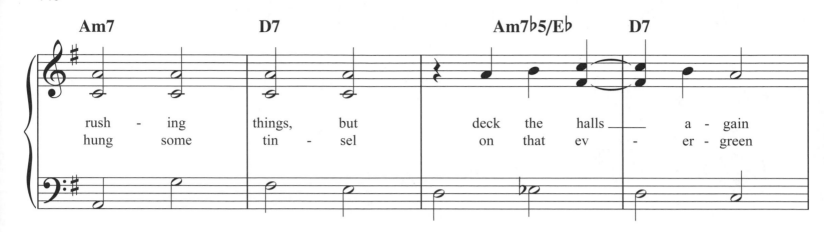

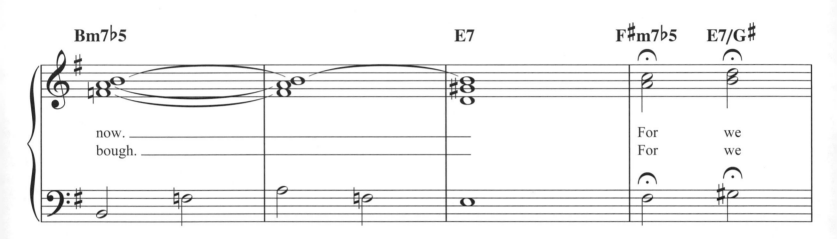

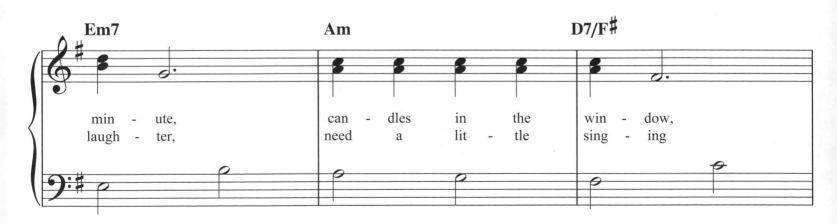

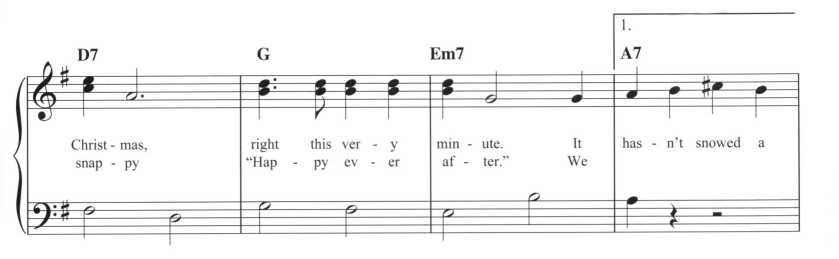

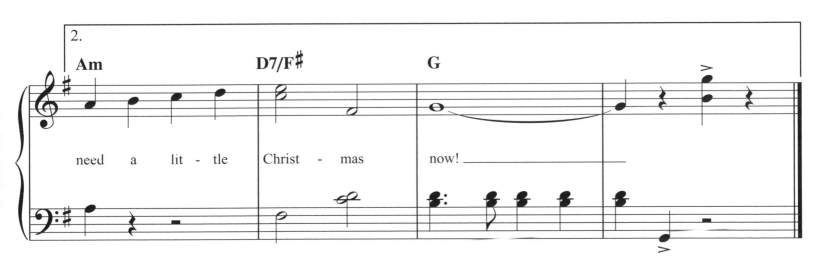

# WHITE CHRISTMAS
### from the Motion Picture Irving Berlin's HOLIDAY INN

Words and Music by
IRVING BERLIN

**Slowly**

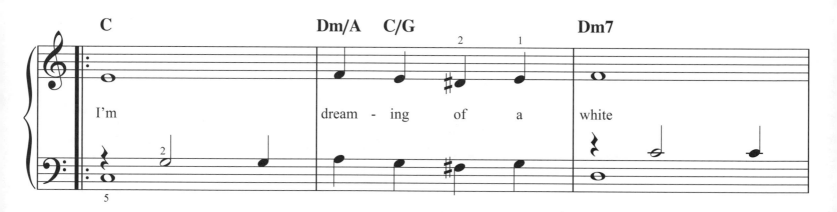

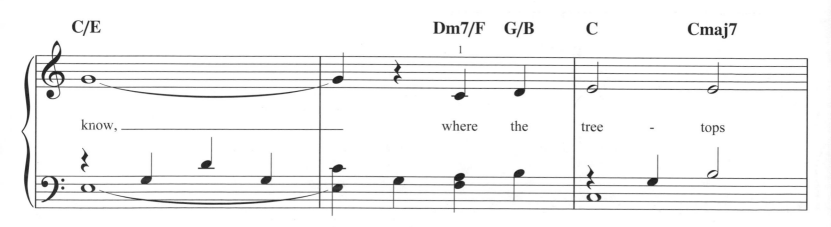

glis - ten and chil - dren lis - ten to hear

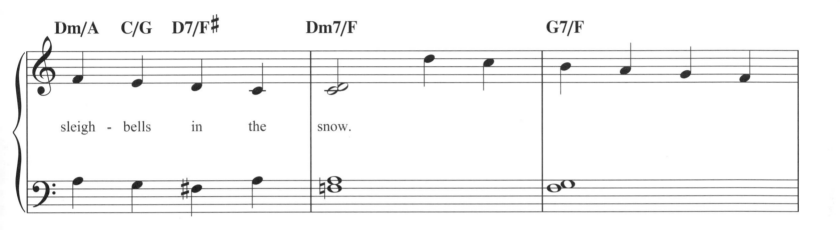

sleigh - bells in the snow.

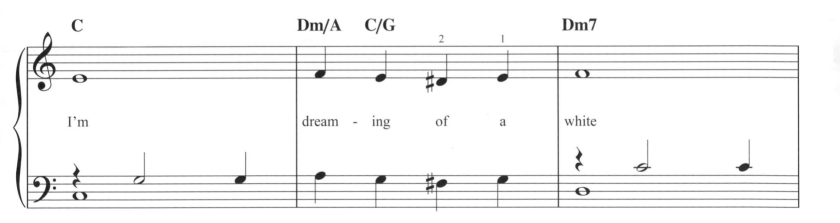

I'm dream - ing of a white

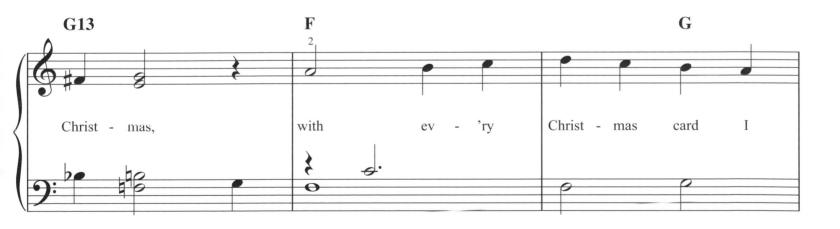

Christ - mas, with ev - 'ry Christ - mas card I

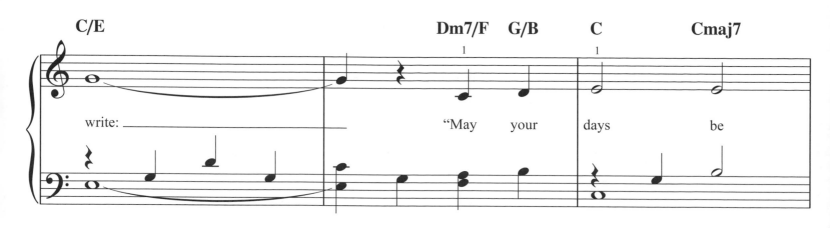

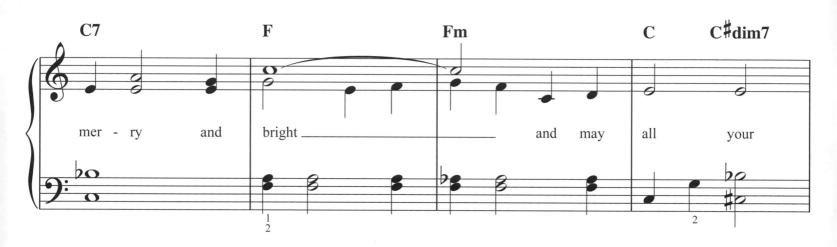

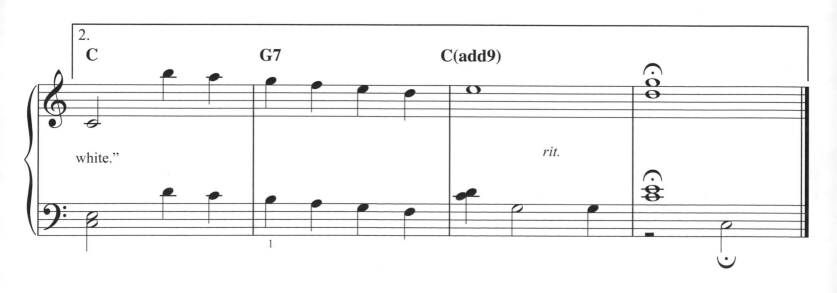

# YOU'RE ALL I WANT FOR CHRISTMAS

Words and Music by GLEN MOORE
and SEGER ELLIS

**Moderately**

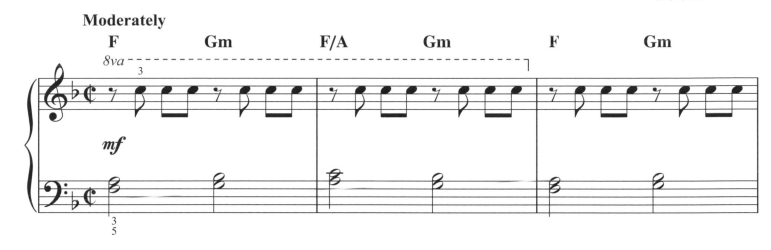

When San - ta comes a - round at Christ - mas time and

leaves a lot of cheer at ev - 'ry door, if he would on - ly grant the

wish in my heart, I would nev - er ask for more. You're

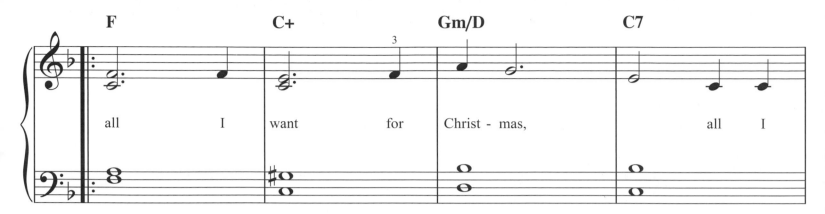

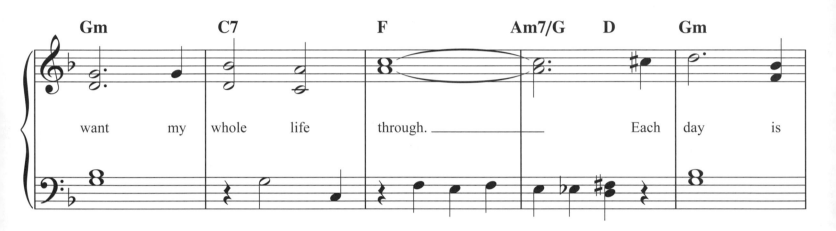

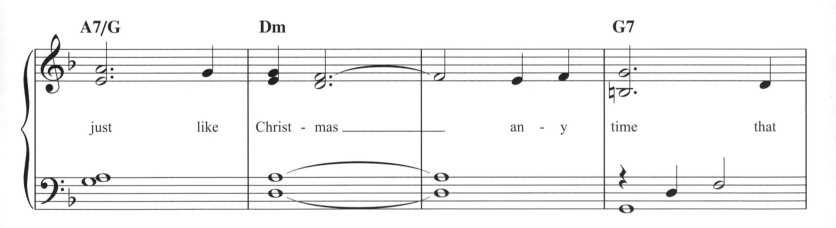

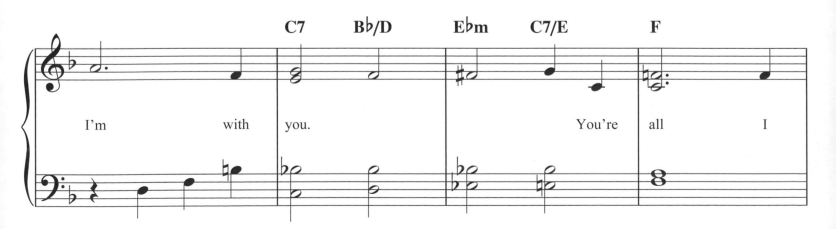

147

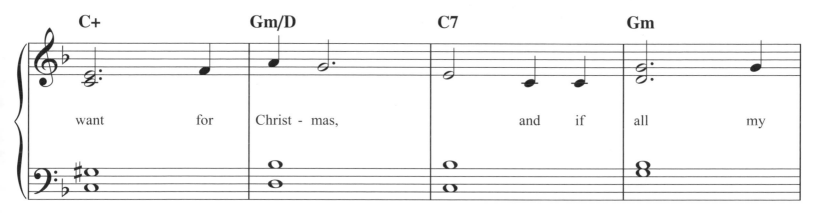

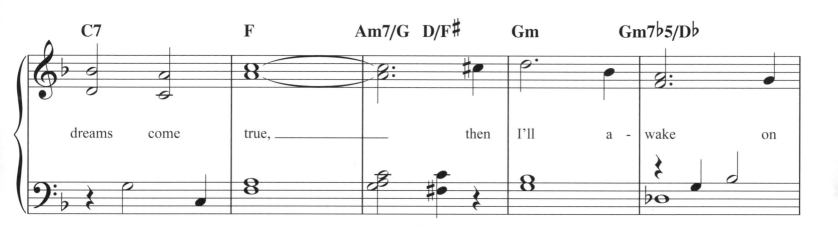

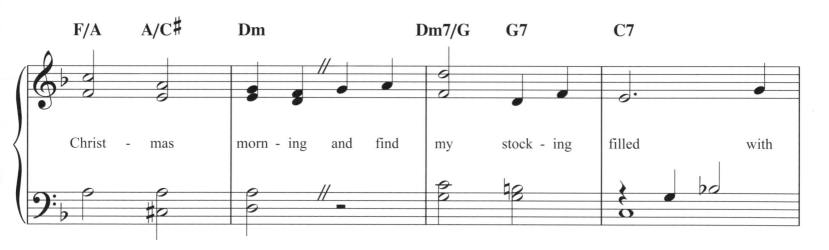

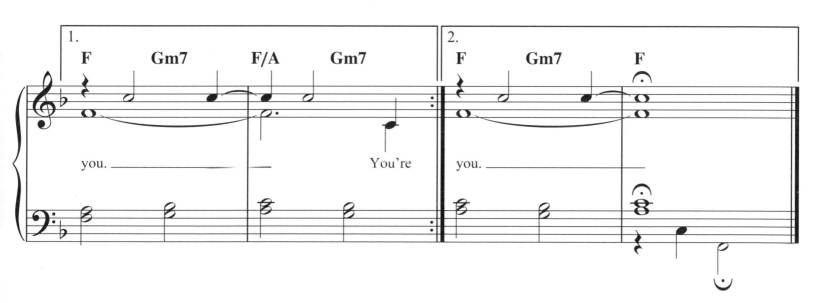

# WINTER WONDERLAND

Words by DICK SMITH
Music by FELIX BERNARD

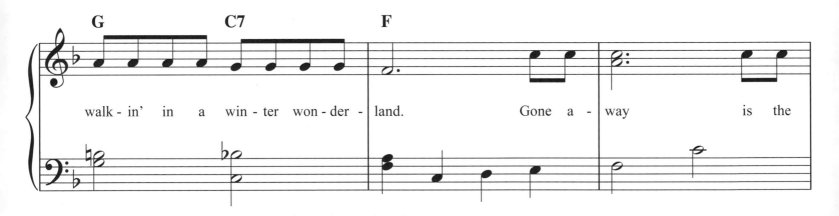

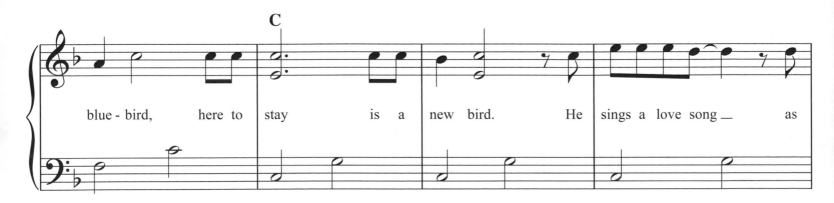

149

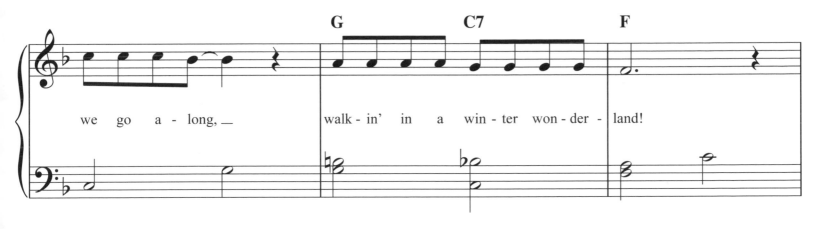

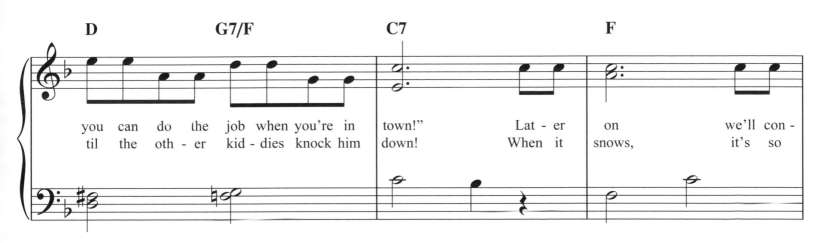

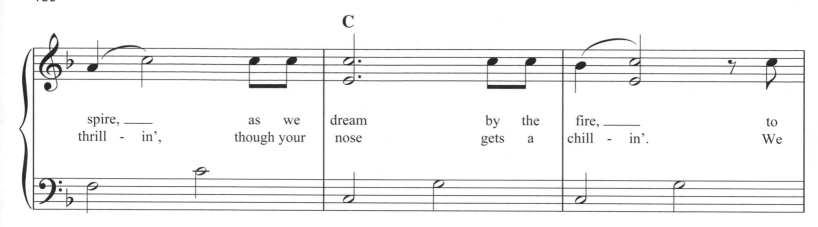

spire, \_\_\_\_\_ as we dream by the fire, \_\_\_\_\_ to
thrill - in', though your nose gets a chill - in'. We

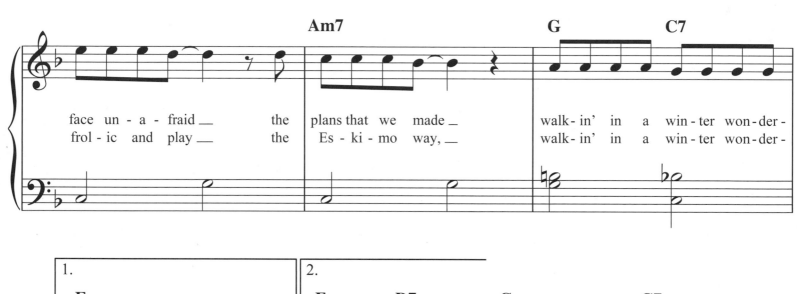

**Am7**      **G**      **C7**

face un - a - fraid \_\_ the plans that we made \_\_ walk- in' in a win - ter won-der-
frol - ic and play \_\_ the Es - ki - mo way, \_\_ walk- in' in a win - ter won-der-

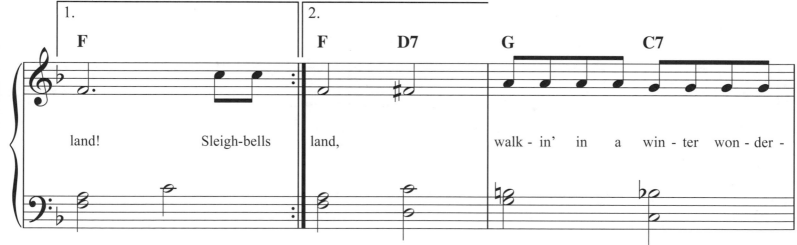

**1.**    **F**      **2.**    **F**    **D7**      **G**      **C7**

land! Sleigh-bells land, walk - in' in a win - ter won-der-

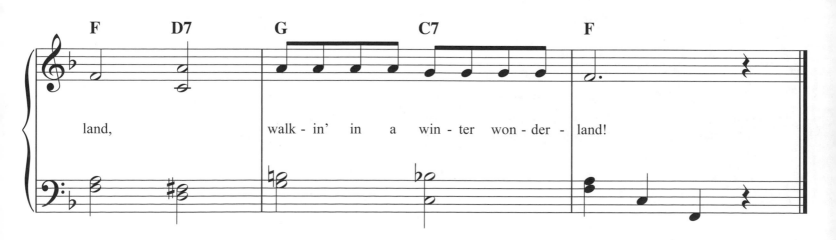

**F**    **D7**      **G**      **C7**      **F**

land, walk - in' in a win - ter won - der - land!